T0365904

# CLEANING THE
# MIRROR

## 365 Inspirations for
## a Course in Miracles

REV. GREGORY WADLEIGH

authorHOUSE®

AuthorHouse™
1663 Liberty Drive
Bloomington, IN 47403
www.authorhouse.com
Phone: 1 (800) 839-8640

Published by AuthorHouse  07/16/2016

ISBN: 978-1-5049-7931-3 (sc)
ISBN: 978-1-5049-7930-6 (e)

Print information available on the last page.

This book is printed on acid-free paper.

Dedicated to the great symbols of God's love in my life;
my wife Debbie, my muse Stephanie, my friend Marley.

Each page of this book is an inspiration drawn from A Course in Miracles. Intended to be helpful in our practice and illustrative of those principles, these pages are offered as extensions of love in hopes of bringing a certain peace.

JANUARY 1ˢᵗ – VIEW - I am seeing. The view from my ego is incorrect. Everything that I see from the perspective of self-centeredness means nothing. Involved in my small self I consistently see things from the perspective of lack. So all that I observe are symbols for a world of lack. Since we really live in an abundant universe all of these observances are untrue. Today I want to begin to change the way that I see. First I will admit that my present vision tends to be in error, and then I will open my mind to a higher understanding. I will ask my inner guide to help my see. I will do this at least twice today; right now and then at the end of the day. I will also try to ask for guidance any time I realize I am caught in my own smallness.

JANUARY 2nd – MEANING - I am interpreting. I give meaning to everything that I perceive. This concept is the beginning of a process that will lead to taking responsibility for life and thus finding freedom. Today let us look more deeply into our own thoughts as they occur; we will see that we are forming our reality out of the opinions stored in our small mind. This revelation will change us to the extent that we embrace it. Our commitment to a life of peace will be evidenced by our on going decisions to treat everything we see as reflections of the past. There is a Part of us that is not concerned with the dead past or the uncertain future and it is that Part we want to relax into.

JANUARY 3rd – UNDERSTANDING - I am clearing the past. Caught in the illusion, which we call the world we have seen everything based on past associations. Because we see things through this filter of the past we do not understand what it is that we see right now. Today let us focus on releasing the past and seeing things in a fresh way. Buddhist teaching calls this beginner's mind. We begin with openness, the mind a blank slate. Admitting that we are not seeing correctly leaves the way open to a new way. Our affirmation can be something like " I am open and receptive to the voice of the Holy Spirit." or "I don't understand this, but the Holy Spirit can illuminate me if I ask." Diligent repetition of these ideas throughout the day will result in new, clearer perceptions.

JANUARY 4th – THOUGHTS - I am thinking. The thoughts we think with the ego are thoughts of lack, which spring from a thought system of lack. These erroneous thoughts have filled our heads for so long that we think they are actually meaningful. They are not. These thoughts are pale reflections of our true thoughts; they are twisted into strange and alien forms as a result of the fear they generate. We can think of them as dark shadows, which obscure the light of our true source. Begin today by taking responsibility for your thoughts. Make a decision to change your mind. Recognizing that these shadow thoughts are not helpful and that they can be changed is a good start. Decide for light, the light that shines beyond the shadows, and the light that dispels the clouds. Stop thinking with the ego and start thinking from your right mind.

JANUARY 5<sup>th</sup> – UPSET - I am aware of upset. In ego, we have adopted a thought system of fear. In Spirit we are letting that system fade while we re-establish ourselves in the thought system of love. Once we recognize that in small self-centeredness we are always upset, we can decide to be otherwise. One of the most important things is to see that all of our various reason for upset are actually not... meaning that what we think has us upset is not the issue. So today, our practice will be one of denial...we will realize that whatever the apparent symptom it is not the reason for our upset. We will tell ourselves "I am not upset (whatever form the upset takes can be substituted) for the reason I think." For now it is not important to be concerned about what the real reason is, but we should be open to any guidance that comes from Spirit as we do these denials.

JANUARY 6th – ILLUSION - I am examining my upsets. Standing back, observing I see that all of my upsets are the same. As I search my mind for a minute I am able to list some upsets. Some are seen to be just minor irritations and others look to be of greater magnitude. They are all obstacles to peace and they are all indicative of the rage that lies just beneath the surface of my ego-mind. I believe that deeper, further inside; I will find that which is real. I will find my true self...if that happens today I am open to it...if not I will try again tomorrow. But today I will make an attempt to see that these upsets are not real...that they are all just symbols for something else. I have been seeing something that is not there...and I have been distracted from the Truth. I am not going to worry about the nature of the upset; I just know that it is not real.

JANUARY 7th – PAST - I am in the present. I am in the present, but I have been seeing only the past. I have been bound by all of my past perceptions. These views have restricted my understanding and have set me up for the suffering that continues in my life. Caught in the past we think from a past perspective. Right now let us begin anew... reminding ourselves that we see only the past; we have reached the point of awareness that will lead to a necessary surrender. As ACIM lesson 7 instructs, we observe the world around us and then admit that we see only the past in it. We realize that the reason we are stuck in a conflict is that what we see is based on past events that are also only illusions. If this is too hard to accept we can just think of our upsets as mistaken perception. Recognition is what we seek today, just acceptance of the fact that we see only the past.

JANUARY 8th – THINKING - I am changing my thinking. I think I am thinking, but really I have just been caught in a loop... The ego has been presenting me with a stream of false thoughts. These thoughts are images of the past. Since the past is gone these thoughts are about something that is "not there". Meaning that all of my thoughts coming through the ego's filter of the past are in error. They are not true and for all intents and purposes they are not real. Today I will notice when I am thinking ego thoughts. I will recognize that no matter what it seems I am thinking about, that I am really just preoccupied with the past. Since these preoccupations are not really thoughts I will consider the idea that I am really not thinking at all. So, when I am caught in this past preoccupation my mind is really blank. The more I make this recognition the closer I will be to the uncovering my true mind and my true thoughts, the closer I will be to living in the present moment.

JANUARY 9th – SEEING - I am seeing differently. When I am caught in the loop of past thoughts, I do not see anything as it is now. Because the ego wants me to be preoccupied with past thoughts it presents me with false perceptions in everything that I think I see. Today, I will open my mind to the present. First I will tell myself that everything I am seeing is an image generated out of past events. I will consider the idea that my physical vision is clouded by all of my prejudices. I will observe my world, telling myself as I do that I do not see anything as it is right now. The intellectual idea is not hard to accept...my seeing is based on what I believe has occurred in the past. Those past experiences color all of my vision. The principle is clear, but the true meaning is obscured because my small self does not want me to really get it. All of my looking has been distracting me. Maybe today, I can only accept the intellectual recognition but I will continue to remind myself knowing that eventually I will see differently.

JANUARY 10th – RELEASE - I am being released from the meaningless. When I realize that my ego's thoughts do not mean anything, I am paving the way to freedom from my erroneous beliefs. Today, I will observe my self-centered thoughts telling myself that they really don't mean anything. Any thought that I have that is based in fear, caught up in the past, or concerned for the future does not mean anything. All thoughts of comparisons, contrasts, judgments do not mean anything. All guilt or shame, resentment or regret does not mean anything. I may have held these particular things as important and meaningful, but I will now tell myself that they and all of their related thoughts do not mean anything. I will remember that this way leads to freedom from my meaningless beliefs.

JANUARY 11th – MEANING - I am meaningful. My thoughts control my sight. The way I think determines what I see in the world. These are not easy ideas to digest. We believe that the things we see in the world are events that we have no control over and that they then are the cause of the way we feel and think. This is actually not so. What is going on inside us projects outside of us to form our vision of the world. Unfortunately we believe that the world is the cause and we (our thinking, feeling, acting) are the effect. That is backwards...our thoughts are the cause and what we see are the effects. For now, just suspend disbelief and consider the possibility. It is actually a very freeing concept. All of our suffering thoughts produce a suffering world. All of our suffering thoughts are actually meaningless thoughts, which show us a meaningless world. Today, remember that even if the world appears meaningless that you are meaningful and you affect the world your see.

JANUARY 12th – MEANINGLESS - I am free from the meaningless world that I have made. When I observe all of the senseless conflict in the world I am afraid. It is important for me to realize that what I see is an expression of my own inner condition. I am afraid because I believe I am alone and under threat. This belief will continue to haunt me until I change it. No one else can do this for me. Today I will commit to changing what I believe. I will begin by quieting the mind. I will then accept the fact that I am in control of the thoughts that arise in my mind. If any thoughts occur which are disquieting I will exchange them for other thoughts. As I do this I will expect that my feelings concerning life and the world will change. Changed feelings will lead to change actions. Soon, I will be free or at least free to think that which I really want to think...surely this will lead to a vision of a changed world.

JANUARY 13th – OPEN - I am open and receptive. Today I will practice mind clearing. I will attempt to go out into the world with my mind being a blank slate. I will not assign meaning to anything I see. I will allow the still small voice within to inform me as to what things mean. When I disagree with that voice, I will suspend my disbelief and act as if the inspiration that I have received is correct. Any thoughts that are contrary to the loving thoughts of spirit will be noted, then released and finally substituted; love for fear. Every time the mind closes I will reopen it. I will be receptive to the voice for God, ignoring the plaintiff cries of the ego. I can surrender any thought of being in conflict or competition with Creation...I can be open and receptive.

JANUARY 14th – RELIEF - I am relieved to know that God did not create suffering. The world I perceive is not God's world. The material world of suffering is the world that I have made. This is a difficult thing to accept because it is much easier to blame God or other people or circumstances or bad luck. Once accepted, however, this personal responsibility actually points to freedom. It reveals the fact that we are indeed in charge of how we see the world, which is really to say how we make the world we see. Any guilt that results from this realization is counter-productive. If God does not create suffering then the next question might be "What does God create?" Well, God creates like himself. God creates love. When I feel apart from God I am apart from Love. Not feeling Love, I suffer...but it is a suffering of my own making. I know that I can choose differently and so I do just that.

JANUARY 15th – IMAGES - I am imaging my world. Today we practice looking at the world with soft eyes. Relax and "un-focus" the eyes, just let them establish a gaze that does not have hard edges. Remind yourself that every image within your vision is a perception being reported to your brain. The way you see the image has everything to do with past experience and future anticipation concerning that image. Consider the idea that there is something beyond what the eyes see. It is important to let these new thoughts enter into consciousness because it is what lies behind the symbols that we seek.

JANUARY 16th – NEUTRAL - I am recognizing. Today I will begin to notice that every thought I have has an impact on my life. Because my thoughts actually build the world that I see; it seems prudent that I try to choose what I think. Every loving thought creates more love; every fearful thought makes more fear. So there really is no neutral thought because each gives either peace or suffering. I want to recognize the affect that my thoughts are having, so I will pay attention throughout the day; just noticing what is going on in me.

JANUARY 17th – SURROUNDINGS - I am attentive. Today, let us remember that just as our thoughts are affecting what we see; that which we see generates more thoughts that in turn affect our feelings. We should ask ourselves what we were thinking when we reacted to something that seemed to happen… we should ask what we believe that generated the thought that triggered the reaction. Surely we will find that we believed that we were alone, and that we then thought that we were in some sort of danger. Pay attention…all of theses thoughts of peril are the result of belief in separation from God. It is an illusion, nothing more… For the rest of the day let us stop acting on this false evidence.

JANUARY 18th – CONNECTED - I am connected. We are connected to one another… our minds are joined at more than one level. When we experience something, that experience is shared. At the level of reality, we are connected. The evidence that is presented to us from the level of the material world would seem to indicate that we are not connected… this is incorrect. Our minds are joined at all levels but are also denying that the connection exists… hence the conflict. Suffice it to say, when we experience something, that experience is shared. Some of these connections are noticed, most are not, but they are happening nonetheless. Today let us try to feel these connections in what we think, say, and do.

JANUARY 19th – SHARED - I am sharing my thoughts. Since minds are joined any thought we have is shared at some level with everyone else. Take some time today to notice this sharing. The phone rings just as you are thinking of someone and on the other end it is he or she. You call someone and they say; "I was just thinking about you!" You have an idea for some kind of product…some solution for a common problem and then soon you see something similar introduced to the marketplace. This is evidence, even in the material world, that minds are joined. We are concerned here with something deeper than that but the symbol of world events can still teach the lesson. Every thought we have goes forth to touch all living things and theirs come to us. Today, just notice these thoughts and allow for a moment that you are not alone in experiencing their effects.

JANUARY 20th – DETERMINED - I am determined to see. We are not being forced to do anything; whatever we decide is totally up to us. Today we can decide for happiness and peace or we can decide for more suffering. If we say we want the best but then choose less than that we are just deceiving ourselves. Right now we are really getting what we want but we can change our minds…that of course takes some discipline. Today just continue to remind yourself that it is possible to see things differently and that you are determined to do so. Coming to a new state of mind is the result.

JANUARY 21st – DIFFERENCE - I am determined to see things differently. Today we will focus on specifics. Each person and situation that seems to be causing anger or distress will be examined. It does not really matter whether they seem to be evoking just a slight annoyance or full-blown upset. They are really all the same. Suffering comes from this upset; indeed it is the upset itself. Anger is felt within and projected out. Internal disturbance looks for external justification. We are really very upset with ourselves, this condition is intolerable so we try to find evidence that all of our problems are caused by people, circumstances and events. Try to be aware that the upset is just a smoke screen which obscures what is really going on…and be determined to see it differently.

JANUARY 22nd – JUDGEMENT - I am correcting my sight. Let me see that all of my judgment is an attack on the world. As we attack the world the world seems to attack back. Buried within the belief system is the thought that we are continually under attack and must therefore defend ourselves…these beliefs are justified every time we look at the material world. It seems quite clear that in the world we are in danger. The facts are slightly different… that since we project our anger out onto the world, the world takes vengeance… that we must in turn respond to… the cycle is set and continues to repeat. Today we are going attempt to break the pattern by deciding that this is not the world we want to see. A change of view is required.

JANUARY 23rd – SURRENDER - I am surrendering. Today we will take our previous decision that we want to correct our sight and move into action. The world of danger that is apparent as we defend ourselves is the world we want to escape. We cannot control the world we see. It is not possible to change it through some wishing or hoping or even some great force of will. The way we will change the world is by stopping our attack thoughts. So, first recognize the attack thought, decide you don't want it and then let it go. When you have another such thought acknowledge it and then give it up, and so on. Remember that it doesn't matter which side of the attack you seem to be on, it is really all the same. Recognize them, decide you don't want them, and then let them go. Notice how the world changes.

JANUARY 24th – PERCEPTION - I am on the path. On this path to a new understanding we begin with the fact that our perception of the world is wrong. We make the world we see through our thoughts, but we also believe that the world is infringing on us. Our decisions and our actions are cause of the effects we see, but we believe the effects are the cause of our happiness or unhappiness. Our perception is incorrect and further we do not know what is best for us. Everything seen through the fog of self-centeredness is incorrect. We believe we know what is best but we do not, because we only think of ourselves alone. Even when we believe we have the best interest of others in mind it is from our own perspective, which is clouded by fear. Today let us ask for help in our decisions, let us surrender our alone-ness and look for guidance from that Power greater than our small selves.

JANUARY 25th – PURPOSE - I am on the path to happiness. We do not know what is best for us. Individually we will always misinterpret the world. We are confused about purpose, everything has a purpose but we do not know what it is. Today let us consider the idea that everything has the purpose of being for our best interest. Every person, every situation, every event, every place, everything is for our best interest. Counter-intuitive as that may seem it is the truth. We rebel against it because we think that "bad" things are against us and that it would be egotistical to think that all "good" things are for our best interest. Our discomfort shows through. Let us realize that in our ego we do not recognize the purpose of anything because we mistakenly believe that it is either with us or against us. Know this: God's will is that everything is for us and with us and all can contribute to our shared happiness.

JANUARY 26th – INVULNERABLE - I am invulnerable. In spirit we are all invulnerable, we cannot be harmed in any way. Only in this material world that we have made can we be hurt. We think we have attacked and therefore we believe we have been and can be attacked. Our worries and anxiety are all attack thoughts. Today let us examine these thoughts; we will admit that we are concerned over, worried about, and afraid of certain possibilities. After considering all the fearful ramifications we will realize that these thoughts are attacks upon ourselves. Invulnerable means "immune from attack", but if we can attack we can be attacked so we must not be invulnerable. What if we did not attack? If we did not attack we would not be attacked. This is not an easy teaching, but it is well worth learning through practice.

JANUARY 27th – DESIRE - I am longing for true sight. Today let us make the seeking of vision a priority. No sacrifice is called for... only a small amount of willingness. To see a world free of suffering is the determination. To image a loving home, neighborhood, community, country and world... then relaxing the boundaries and the borders... to act kindly, to think harmoniously, to believe in the unity of all life... this is true vision and the only worthy goal. Be willing and determined to see correctly.

JANUARY 28th – CHANGE - I am willing to change. Today let us commit to changing the way we see the world. Make this change the most important goal of the day. Release the past... release pre-conceived ideas... release preference... be open-minded to the present moment. In all that occurs today ask to be shown the true meaning of each noticed thing. Realize that the true nature, the true purpose of all things is to reunite all into oneness. Everything animate or inanimate is pointing the way back to wholeness.

JANUARY 29th – EVERYTHING- I am loving. Today we begin to see differently. Let us consider the idea that God actually is present. As we say every Sunday at One Spirit Center: "We see God everywhere, in everyone, and in everything." The question is "Do we?" What we are really trying to do is to see past the images we have made. These images that we call various things actually obscure our view of Reality, which is to say God. Really all of these images are just symbols. They can be symbols of separation or they can be symbols for Unity. We decide: look with love or look with fear, look with appreciation or look with criticism. Opening our minds to the possibility that the Divine lies just beyond the mundane will be a great help.

JANUARY 30th – MIND - I am joining. Today could be an end to the projection of guilt. We have the opportunity to stop seeing what we do not want. We will try to join with life rather than find reasons to be alone. Our practice will be to look at the world with eyes of love, allowing for the possibility that all that actually exists is God. Further that all life arises and extends from the mind of God. We, being the creation of God are also part of all that there is. Invest everything in everything…give love to life.

JANUARY 31st – RESPONSIBLE - I am responsible. We are free, which means we are responsible. We will stop thinking of ourselves as being at the mercy of circumstances and events. If anything goes wrong during the day remember that we get to decide what to do next. The weather does not have to affect us, a disappointment at work does not have to dictate our mood, a seeming slight from an associate does not have to be a commentary on our worth, and a financial setback does not have to hold us back. Anything that happens that seems to threaten us in any way can be put into proper perspective by realizing that we choose what we will do next.

FEBRUARY 1st – INVENTION - I am creative. Being the child of God we inherit creation and the ability to create. Being attached to our ego identity in the material world our creativity is but a shadow of what it is in Reality, but we still make the world we see. Sometimes that which we make seems very good indeed at other times it seems quite distressing. It is important for us to remind ourselves that these experiences are not being done to us but rather that we are calling them into our lives… sometimes we do this consciously but mostly it is unconscious. Sometimes we seem to be making "it" on our own but really we are always conspiring with our brothers and sisters to continue this perception of separation. Once we accept the fact that we are inventing the world, we can set about changing the experience.

FEBRUARY 2nd – SHIFT - I am shifting my perspective. Let us put our decision-making ability to work today. Sit quietly for a moment and allow yourself to reflect on your current condition; consider that which seems to be going on outside yourself and also that which is happening on the inside. Whatever thoughts come to mind treat them all the same… if a certain situation seems unpleasant and another seems pleasant know that both of them can be seen differently. As you examine each event on the screen of your mind's eye just remind yourself in a very neutral way that there is another way of seeing it. Then allow whatever changes come next to naturally occur without fighting them, but remember that those new images can also be seen differently.

FEBRUARY 3rd – PEACE - I am seeking… Peace is what we seek. We are told that: "It is from your peace of mind that a peaceful world perception arises." Throughout the day as different events seem to occur remember that there is another way of looking at them and that way can lead to peace. In ACIM workbook lesson 34 it is suggested that when any adverse emotions are felt to simply look at the situation, which seems to be causing them and say, "I could see peace instead of this." This practice will be most helpful today and will continue to be a balm of healing in the years ahead. No matter how distressful the matter may be it will be improved significantly by looking for peace in the midst of it. The effort will have a benefit even if total peace does not result. Keep practicing and the goal of peace will be sure.

FEBRUARY 4<sup>th</sup> – MIND - I am part of God. Specifically our minds are part of Mind. ACIM tells us that we are very holy and that this holiness is the result of being part of the mind of God. So, we are really in God and not really in the world. Difficult as this idea is to accept it is true. It is for this change of perspective that we are practicing. To go from the notion of being outside in the world, to a knowing that really we are inside the mind of God… this is our path to peace. The second idea that logically stems from this one is "If we are part of God's mind and God is Holy then we must be Holy too. Consider Holiness for a moment and notice any upset or disbelief or rebellion that arises. No need to fight these thoughts, just note them and go back to considering the possibility that all this time we have been wrong about our place in the universe that we are not on the outside at all but rather on the very Holy Inside.

FEBRUARY 5th – ENVELOP - I am enveloped in the Love of God. Further, as part of God we are also capable of enveloping all that we see in holiness and love. In ACIM lesson 36 is the idea introduced that not only are we Holy but that holiness means that we are sinless. If this concept causes concern just note the concern and continue to examine and explore the ideas of holiness and being sinless. For today let us just act as if these things are true and then put them into action by visualizing the holy light in us extending out into the world. As the Course suggests see this holy light extending to and enveloping whatever is perceived. Try to do this with a sense of peace, feel the love that is extending and know that it can never be lost or extinguished.

FEBRUARY 6ᵗʰ – BLESSING - I am blessing the world. Wow! What a shock. We may have thought of ourselves as being very bad and therefore very guilty or just somewhat good and somewhat bad…neither doing much good or too much bad…but here we are presented with a different role: the role of being a blessing. Wandering through life experiencing alternate states of feeling "less than" or "greater than" is not our purpose. Our purpose is to bless the world we see. Sacrifice is not called for, there can be no loss in this giving. Everyone will gain and no one will lose. If everyone gains then we gain, if nobody loses then we cannot lose. Today we will exercise our purpose by consciously blessing all that we see and all that we think about. Visualize the holiness within going forth to fill the perceived gap between us and further, to totally enfold us. Our blessing returns to bless us, now and forever.

FEBRUARY 7th – UNLIMITED - I am unlimited. After feeling inadequate much of the time, today's idea could be disturbing. Recognize any distress and then quietly let it go and move into the mindset that because you are part of God's mind you are very holy and that there is nothing that your holiness cannot do. Notice that it does not say that there is nothing that "your ego" cannot do. There is nothing that your holiness cannot do. Your holiness is the divine in you, it is your true identity…it is not the ego. The application of this principle can be quite specific. Any problem that may be on your mind can start to be put right with an affirmation concerning the fact that there is nothing that your holiness cannot do. There is nothing that "you" have to do, just affirm the power of your holiness and then let that power go to work for you.

FEBRUARY 8th – SAFE - I am safe. We are safe and sound in the mind of God. Our holiness is our safety. All of the perceived dangers in the world arise from our own deep guilt. As hard as this may be to believe right now it is nonetheless true. Rather than look for arguments, just allow for the possibility and use the idea today. Our guilt is both conscious and subconscious. On the surface we are guilty about our thoughts and actions, we project that guilt onto others and then are in turn guilty about that. Beneath the surface we are guilty about leaving God…this is the cause of all suffering and is indeed the very definition of hell. ACIM lesson 39 suggests that: "My unloving thoughts are keeping me in hell. My holiness is my salvation." So today let us put our holiness into action by releasing unloving thoughts and then extending loving ones.

FEBRUARY 9th – HAPPY - I am happy. Being the child of a loving God means being heir to the Kingdom. This is our true condition...we in a state of grace. We are heirs to peace. We are blessed with an abundance of all good things. Say to yourself: I am loved and I am loving. Spirit fulfills me. I am blessed; therefore I will be a blessing. Today will be a day of calm as we consider our position of safety within the mind of God. Anytime we find ourselves becoming anxious or upset let us return to one of these affirmations. We can establish quiet confidence by remembering that we have access to the strength of God. All that is good (of God) is also of us...this should be the source of great happiness.

FEBRUARY 10th – PRESENCE - I am in the Presence. We are present in God. God is present in us. Let us remember throughout the day "God goes with us wherever we go". This principle of being all one is a comfort whenever we feel that we are alone. Since we live and move and have our being in God it is actually impossible for us to be alone. Regardless of this reality we may from time to time believe that we are on our own. The more we identify with the body the more we will feel this isolation. Fortunately we can get relief, even in the material world, by reminding ourselves that actually we are with God and God is with us wherever we go.

FEBRUARY 11th – STRENGTH - I am strong. The strength of God is our strength. How often, how long will we forget? In our small separated self the ego alternately rages and quivers. The ego feels inadequate but tries to feign superiority; is afraid but projects a false courage that is really aggression. It is in spirit that we find our true powers. Strength and sight are two of the things we receive when we relax into the arms of spirit. From this safe vantage point we can see what is ours to do and find the power to do it. Because we are strong we are able to be truly helpful. From this strength and vision we are able to do the right thing for the right reason at exactly the right time.

FEBRUARY 12th – SOURCE - I am flowing from God. God is the fount from which we flow. It may seem as if we are bodies in competition with other bodies for limited resources. In truth we are all flowing together from God and also in this flow is all that we have need of. The various sights we see in the material world are false evidence appearing real...true vision, the real view, comes only from spirit and is not of the material world. When we relax, when we center ourselves in love, we begin to sense the true nature of life. Abundance is our birthright and is available to us all. When this idea is held in mind, it produces prosperity in the world we see.

FEBRUARY 13<sup>th</sup> – LIGHT - I am in the light. We are in the light, but the light that we are in is actually on the Inside not the outside. We should remember that there really is no outside...the outside is the illusion. The light on the inside will wash away the shadows on the outside. The light in us gives us the ability to see the symbols on the outside correctly. Take a moment now to step aside from emotion, let go of any worries or concerns...release any grievances... allow yourself to sink deeply into the peace that lies within you. Observe...just observe...try to not have any attachment to beliefs, thoughts or emotions that may present themselves. Just notice them and gently let them go. If any sense of discomfort should arise just repeat the affirmation "I am in the light". Notice the sense of peace that now permeates your mind...know that this is your natural condition. Continue as long as possible and then repeat later in the day.

FEBRUARY 14ᵗʰ – MIND - I am in the mind of God. We exist as thoughts in the mind of God. This Mind is also the mind in which our true thoughts exist and extend into creation. The thoughts that we are having in the ego are thoughts of getting and grasping, thoughts of lack and emptiness. The thoughts we are having in the mind of God are thoughts of Love and Light. The ego thoughts pull a curtain across the loving thoughts...the ego obscures what is real and presents that which will forever be unreal. In other words the ego lies and fabricates...it makes a world of trouble and hides the real world. Today we make an attempt to release the ego thoughts without having any emotional attachment to them...we simply notice them, admit they are not correct and then ask Spirit to show us what is real. That's it! Simple. Let us do this throughout the day whenever we notice that the worldly thoughts are interfering with our peace.

FEBRUARY 15th – LOVE - I am the love of God in action. The action we take in the world will either hurt or heal. If we act from the fear that the ego generates we will experience and promote hurt. When we act from unity and love we will contribute to the healing of all of the ego's fear. Regret and resentment make a world of pain; forgiveness erases all of the pain along with its cause. Remember that God is not mad at you. You are mad at you...so say to yourself: "Through the love of God in me, I forgive all of our mistakes". Observe what happens as you become willing to let go of all regret for your own past actions and then to release all resentment against your brothers and sisters. Our forgiveness of the world is the mission...it is indeed the action we take to experience the love of God in us.

FEBRUARY 16th – TRUST - I am trusting. Living on the surface of life we are buffeted by the waves of fear and the winds of change. From the ego's perspective we are not up to the task of negotiating these dangerous waters. We are afraid of all of the seeming dire possibilities. In our suffering we have put our faith in the things of the material world; this trust in outer conditions will surely result in continued pain. Today, let us put our trust in God and go beneath the stormy surface of our minds, let us sink quietly beyond the reach of our small self. Deeper, deeper we go into the peace that passes understanding. Deep into our true selves we find that place of perfect peace that the Course identifies as "the Kingdom of Heaven". Yes, the Kingdom of Heaven, not somewhere overhead or in some far off dimension but rather within us. Rest here a little while today, stay a moment in Heaven, experience the place of perfect peace that is always within in us.

FEBRUARY 17th – TRUTH - I am relying on truth. The weakness of the ego can be relinquished in favor of the strength of God. We can trust that God is with us wherever we go and we can rely on that Strength in every situation. If we remember that these are actually choices that we make, we can certainly remember to make the correct choice. Throughout the day let us remind ourselves "There is nothing to fear." Anytime we are beset with worries or concerns, whenever we are caught in fear and anger we can say, "There is nothing to fear". Say it and then consider the ramifications of the statement. We are safe and sound in God; we have strayed from Heaven only in our dreams. We can rely on the truth that right here, right now there is nothing to fear.

FEBRUARY 18th – LISTEN - I am listening. We are always listening...identifying with the body we listen to the ego... identifying with spirit we listen to God's voice. The Holy Spirit is the voice for God. ACIM lesson 49 tells us "It is quite possible to listen to God's Voice through the day without interrupting your regular activities in any way". So today let us set the stage for Spirit. Take a moment to get quiet, allow yourself to be calm. Rest in the safety of God, whom you have never really left. Be sure that God goes with you wherever you seem to go and in whatever you do. From this point of view we can see that any work, any task can be done with love. If we keep still we will hear the Voice for God guiding us in all of our endeavors.

FEBRUARY 19th – SUSTAIN - I am sustained. It is easy for us to think that we are sustained by the things of the material world. Our fear of lack is constantly trying to assert its limited view of the world. The thought system of the ego is always looking for evidence that the things we want and need are going to be taken or withheld from us. All of these desires of the ego are substitutes for the only thing we really need: the love of God. Let us establish a vision right now that we are sustained by God. Picture yourself perfectly safe, connected to all life, loved by all life, loving all life, being totally supported by the Love of God. This is the sustenance of Spirit, the abundance of plenty, which is being provided to us at all times and in all places.

FEBRUARY 20th – RELEASE - I am letting go. Today we will continue our practice of letting go of preconceived ideas. Remember that what we see in the material world does not mean anything in Reality. We have invested all that we see with any value it contains for us. Understanding is lost as a result of judgment against the present using evidence from the past. The thoughts that generate as effects of this faulty judgment are further misperceptions. They are upsetting but not for the reason(s) we think. So, let us just let go of every disturbing image...admit to it, realize it is not really true, and let it go.

FEBRUARY 21st – REAL - I am real. Know that any upset that comes today will be the result of seeing things that are not really there. Reality is of God and not anything less. Our judgment of the past which we drag with us into the present keep us from living here and now...our willingness to forgive will be a blessing to all and an escape from suffering. Time is an assault on that which is actually unassailable. Let us choose to be in the present moment so we may see that which is real. All through the day, we can decide to be present by opening our minds to sharing what is real.

FEBRUARY 22nd – THINK - I am thinking. Thinking that we are alone or thinking thoughts that point to separation are exercises in illusion. We cannot be alone because there is no actual place that alone-ness is possible. There is only Mind. There is only the Mind we share with God and with all life. When we get caught in the illusion of the material world we are afraid because we can't understand the impossible. We have made up this strange world, we are in conspiracy with our brothers and sisters to maintain it, and we will suffer until we realize that if God did not make it, it does not exist. Every thought we have in which we imagine ourselves as bodies in competition with other bodies is meaningless. Any thought we have which affirms our Oneness with all Life is a reflection of reality.

FEBRUARY 23rd – EXPERIENCE - I am choosing my experience. We are presented with a clear choice: either change our thinking or continue to get what we really don't want. The suffering of the world we see is our own suffering...it is a reflection of the very thoughts that we have about ourselves. When we decide for thoughts of unity, we activate thoughts of unity in our brothers and sisters. Our thoughts become the lessons that we learn and teach. So, today let us choose to teach love by extending love and thereby experiencing love and ultimately learning love.

FEBRUARY 24ᵗʰ – SIGHT - I am focused. Evidence will be presented today, it will point to guilt, and shame. The picture will trigger fear; it will be false evidence, but will appear to be real. With a little willingness we can focus on the reality that lies hidden behind the symbols that the ego presents. The danger the world shows us can be transformed by love. This transformation requires only one thing: that we give up our own vengeance. Our best interest is the common welfare, what's best for all involved. All of the parts and pieces of this seemingly fragmented world can come to together right now if we just see that really the purpose of everything is for our best interest. Let us give up our vengeance to find peace.

FEBRUARY 25th – INTROSPECTIVE - I am looking within. Today we move toward discovering who we really are. All of the terms we use to describe ourselves are limited concepts that can do nothing but obscure our identity. We have put much energy into building and maintaining our self-concept, which is actually our own prison. We have traded glory for a dark and lonely cell. All of the images we have made hide the fact that there is only God and that which God has created. Of course this is who we really are, creations of God, part of God. Specifically we are thoughts in the mind of God. Our mind is God's mind, God is in our mind and we are in God's mind...because all is Mind.

FEBRUARY 26th – CONSTRUCTION - I am building the world I see. We are not at the mercy of appearance. We actually control the way the world looks to us; by our thoughts we build that world. We have total freedom to see it all differently. Choosing our thoughts chooses our experience. We are not bound by past thoughts because we can decide to think differently now. Any situation we seem to be trapped in can be changed right now simply by thinking about it differently. We can actually transform stress into peace. This is the power of Mind, which is our power to do with what we will. So, we can ask ourselves throughout the day: "What do I want to build?"

FEBRUARY 27th – HOLY - I am holy? Difficult an idea as it may seem, this is the ultimate truth behind all of our practice. Our holiness is the antidote to all of our guilt; it is the solution to all of our various dilemmas. Stop for a moment, close your eyes, and visualize the light of your true identity extending out from you to enfold everything that comes to mind. Realize that this light is Holy Love and that as you extend it you anoint the entire world. Know that nothing is impossible for this Love. Your holiness holds you safe and sound regardless of appearance. It is your blessing but it only blesses by including everyone in its Light.

FEBRUARY 28th – TOGETHER - I am with God. Apart from God...that cannot be. Conflicted, we have believed in error that we stand apart from Creation. Let us put an end to this misconception right now. Today we will see the truth, the truth that we are always with God. God goes with us wherever we go. God is our strength in all that we do. God is the source from which we flow. God is the light, which illumines our path. God is the Mind with which we think. All through the day we will remind ourselves that we are not alone...that truly we can never be alone.

MARCH 1st – EXIST - I am supported by Life itself. We exist within the Love of God. We have a purpose in life and that purpose is to forgive the world. There will be times when it will seem impossible to carry out our purpose, but there is strength in us that we can trust. When we access that strength we will know that there is nothing to fear. Our inner guide, which we might call the Holy Spirit, is the Voice for God which instructs us at all times and in all places. It is this voice, speaking the language of love, which gives direction to our own words and actions. How comfortable would we be if we knew that the whole of Creation is maintaining us? Just consider the possibility that the whole universe is nourishing us right now.

MARCH 2nd – FUNCTION - I am light. Our function in the world is illumination. Let us consider how it works: first we must know we are illuminated...we can feel the light in our heart expanding to fill the body... we can visualize our mind illumined, our spirit ablaze with the light of love. After a few minutes of reflection on these images begin to extend the light out into the world. You may want to send it to some specific people or a situation, that is fine, go ahead. After a few more moments go farther, see your light going forth to bless more and more of the world until you have embraced and enfolded everyone and everything in your forgiveness. Now you know that this is your task, your responsibility and your joyful function.

MARCH 3rd – FORGIVE - I am forgiving. Attack must end in order for us to find peace. It seems such a simple idea, just common sense really. We tend to think that if others would just act right, then we could settle down and find some quiet. This, of course, will never happen as long as we continue to judge. Attack must end with us; we must learn to exchange attack thoughts for loving thoughts. Every time we attack we actually weaken our own position. We can start right now strengthen ourselves by extending love rather than judgment. Practice like this: anytime an uncharitable thought comes to mind just stop for a moment, don't do anything... examine the thought... see that all of these reactions are made by choice and that this type of thinking is suffering... decide (choose) to think something else...something in which everyone involved is set free from suffering. Do this practice as often as possible today and take notice of the differences.

MARCH 4th – PEACE - I am a peacemaker. Today let us not put any goal ahead of this, our most worthy intention. Any other pursuit followed at the expense of peace leaves us all in a poorer state. To accept the mission of peacemaker is to make peace our own. Breathe, relax, feel peace becoming real on the inside... as it grows we will begin to be aware that this peace has always been available to us... further, that it will always be with us... peace only requires our attention and the desire for it. Once established in our minds we can turn to the task of bringing this peace out into the world. Nothing complicated is required, just feel the peace... know that we are centered in peace... see that our center is expanding to encircle all of those around us... everywhere.

MARCH 5th – REMEMBER - I am remembering. Practicing in this way we will eventually remember our true place in God. These lessons are but signposts along the way, of course the more we practice the more time will be saved. Today we remember our function of forgiveness, in which we are a light unto all who come our way. So we remind ourselves now that the ego is incorrect in its assessment of us. Spirit tells us we are one with our source and all of the deception of the ego telling us otherwise should be ignored. We are quite capable of the task, the idea that such a lofty goal could not possibly be ours may be hard to accept but that will not change that fact of our divine mission. Remember we are one with the One.

MARCH 6th – SHINE - I am shining. Our practice for today begins with visualization. Start with the familiar idea that there is a light in you, and see that light shine. Notice how when you focus on this light it grows. It grows to fill your body and then it spills out of your body...the light goes forth to mix and merge with anyone who may be physically near...it is here that the "I" becomes "We". Observe that now we are shining together to extend healing love out into the world...see that that light to all living things now connects us. This is our only responsibility, to complete our function, to see the light in us connected to the light in all.

MARCH 7th – HAPPY - I am happy. When we fulfill our purpose we find happiness. The ego continues to present alternative goals to us, each of these goals come with a promise of happiness. The ego always promises that which it will not or cannot deliver. Always distracting us from what is really important and never fulfilling its promises. Let us stop listening to ego's lies. For a moment see yourself radiant, feel yourself sharing the love of God... get a sense of magnitude of this service... truly the only task worthy of your undivided attention. How does it feel? Happy...it feels happy! This is what happens when we actually perform our function. As the ACIM lesson says: "Our happiness and function are one".

MARCH 8th – LOVE - I am love. When the Bible says we are created in the image of God it is giving us a strong hint of the truth. It is not that God made a cheap copy of Himself, but rather a perfect representation of the divine. The only difference is the order: first Creator then created. God is love and has created us as Love. There is no attribute of the creator that the created do not share. Say: "God is Love and I am loving. God is Light and I am illumined. God is Strength and I am strong." Any quality we can connect to God also resides in us...not in our ego, not in our personality, but in our true identity of spirit.

MARCH 9th – RELEASE - I am letting go. Today we let go of past regret and resentment into a new way of seeing ourselves. Regret conflicts the mind, resentment divides us from one another. Take a moment to review any present regrets, let them go saying, "I have learned from the mistakes of the past and will not repeat them." Next allow yourself to consider those you hold in resentment. Allow willingness to forgive into your heart, hear yourself saying to them: "You are my friend, my brother (sister), really you are myself, I would forgive the past and remember the truth." Take as much time with these exercises as you can...notice how feelings change.

MARCH 10<sup>th</sup> – DISCERN - I am discerning the truth. Allow that we now have some willingness and even some practice concerning letting go of the past. Distorted images will still come to mind, but we are quicker to release them. Let us realize that as ACIM lesson 69 says "Grievances hide the light of the world in me." Each time we practice releasing the past, we will see the present more clearly. Consider once again our true identity (Light), our true nature (Love), and our true place (Heaven). This is reality that will be revealed as our mission proceeds. Throughout the day attempt to discern the light that is within all of us from that which is incorrect.

MARCH 11th – SAFE - I am safe and sound. That which lies within keeps us safe. There is nothing that appears on the outside that can harm us. Let us not be confused by the danger the body feels, after all the body is temporary and that is the cause of its fear. We are not our bodies; we are spirit seeming to have a bodily experience. Envision the entire universe, whole and complete, existing within us. Eternity is within us and we are forever safe in Eternity. Do not be concerned if these visions seem far-fetched, hard to believe or even disturbing...just continue to focus on them as often as possible today.

MARCH 12th – DIRECTION - I am following direction. Let us listen for the guidance we know is there...the guidance of Spirit. There will be a set of directions given today that is dynamic, it will have a foundation in love and be based on forgiveness. The instructions will always be available when they are needed and they are the only ones that will work for our Unifying purpose. The ego, of course, will also speak. It will make promises concerning some solution that is to be found in the material world... ego will speak to self-centeredness and fear will be its message. Today, let us ask for and choose to listen to the guidance from the still small voice and ignore the voice for suffering.

MARCH 13th – WELCOME - I am open. Today let us open our hearts to Love. Closed mind, closed heart...this is the condition that self-centeredness flourishes in. The ego presents its insane approach to life that tells us that aggression brings peace, which keeps us safe from attack. We know that this is not correct but still we find ourselves in circumstances that seem to demand defense/offense. Let us remember that we have a choice. It is a simple choice: hold regrets and resentments and thereby fight what is in our own best interest or we can see things differently and allow a healing miracle to occur. Be open.

MARCH 14th – WILL - I am willing. There is a seeming war of wills in us. Self-will is loud in its demands, always looking for something on the outside to fill the hole it has on the inside. Self-will seems real but it is a fabrication built with all the various fears generated by a thought system of lack. Yet it stands as a choice, it presents its wishes as valid alternatives and even promises rewards for following those wishes. Standing opposite is Goodwill (God's will), which we understand to be what is best for everyone involved. Goodwill is what is in our own best interest which means what is in all of our best interest. Our power of will stands between and allows us to make the choice between the two. Today, let us choose Goodwill.

MARCH 15th – GOODWILL - I am aligned. Let us align ourselves with Goodwill. What if we knew that the will for things, the will for attention, the will for revenge, the will for anything other than Good was just a smokescreen that hides our true will? Any conflict we feel is because we haven't accepted the fact that God's will really is our own true will for ourselves. Just take a moment right now to consider these things: God's will is for peace. In the peace of God there is nothing that can harm us in any way, no upset, no distress, no suffering and no danger. Is Peace not the state we long for? What then is our will other than the longing of our hearts? Our will and God's will all one... remember there is no will but Goodwill and anything else is just an illusion.

MARCH 16th – HEAL - I am healed. Health and wholeness go together; when we are healthy we are peacefully integrated within ourselves and with others. The insanity of separation keeps us sick. This ailment of the mind reflects out into the world we see. Today all of the misperceptions can end. Take a moment to get quiet. Become aware of any ideas that are less than peaceful. Just notice them without any emotional attachment. Tell yourself that these disturbances are just misperceptions that can be healed, relax and see the loving light of God wash over each and every fear. You are being healed right now… remember that healing on the inside will surely show itself on the outside.

MARCH 17th – LAW - "I am under no law but God's". This quote, which comes directly for ACIM lesson 76, describes the natural order of things. God's law is the law of love, the law of extension and the law of creation. These three are really all one and they are the reality of spirit. In the material world we have many insane ideas of what will bring safety. We think if we had a certain amount of money, or possessions, or friends, or even lovers… then everything would be ok. We have found that even if these conditions are met that we still do not feel truly safe. That is because we have designed the world to be dangerous and we continue to fortify that position. The only way out of the fear is to realize that we are not really in this world. Our home is in God, that is what is real, and there we are safe to love and to extend that love into creation.

MARCH 18th – MIRACLES - I am miraculous. Wow! The ego wants to pounce on this statement seeing it as yet another flight of fancy. Miracles are our right and our responsibility. The ability to see a fearful situation differently, to see through to the Love that lies beyond the circumstance that is a gift that has long been given us. Anytime something seems to occur that causes distress, we can move to miracle mindedness. We admit our apparent difficulty, realize that we are making up all of our reactions to the problem, and then visualize a state in which there is no suffering for us or anyone else. This is the miracle of forgiveness that we receive when we take the responsibility to give. Tell yourself that you are miraculous and then go around seeing things differently…

MARCH 19th – REPLACE - I am replacing grievances with miracles. God's will is continually offering us the opportunity for good. At every turn in the road, at every moment of decision we are being given the chance to receive the results of Goodwill which is nothing but good. We actually decide each moment whether we will take offense or whether we will receive love. All of the images that we make concerning other people or the world itself that engender fear (anger, resentment, jealousy, envy) form a shield that we believe protects us from danger but actually block us from experiencing the love of God. So today we will practice lowering the barrier. Whenever a thought that reflects fear comes across our minds we can stop and say "I do not want this thought." We can then release it and replace it with something we really want.

MARCH 20th – SOLUTION - I am in the solution. There is only one problem in the world and in our lives. It seems as if there are many problems…there are money problems, work problems, health problems, and on and on. All of these problems are really relationship problems and they are all really different aspects of the one problem: self-centeredness. The only problem in the world and in our lives is self-centeredness…it is the state of mind that tells us that we are alone and that we are in danger of not getting what we need or losing what we have. The one problem seems to have multiple solutions, all of which involve us getting something we think we want. There really is only one solution to this one problem and that is Love that unites us.

MARCH 21st – FREEDOM - I am free. We are free because all of our problems have already been solved. The one problem which has resulted in many seeming problems is solved! The moment, way back before we can remember or even fully conceive of, that we decided that we were separate from God the answer was instantly provided. Our suffering only continues because we refuse to accept the solution. The only way out of this dilemma is to recognize that we are in it, to realize we don't have to stay in it, and then (and this is the key to our release) extend love into the situation in order to escape it. Love continually presents itself as the solution, let us accept this love now, that we might give it away in order to keep it.

MARCH 22nd – LIGHT - I am lighting up the world. Today, we remember that we are assigned the role of Light. God has designated that we be a light unto everyone and everything that comes to us. This may seem like a burden and indeed it is to the ego. To paraphrase Jesus, this is a burden that is light. To go further with the idea we can see ourselves yoked together with our brothers and sisters by this light. No toil, just joyously sharing the light we are blessed with by forgiving anything that we observe as being dark. So our job is to take the light to the dark, or better yet to give the dark to the light and watch as dark just ceases to be. An easy visualization: see yourself carrying all of your dark burdens out from where you think you hide them and watch as they are healed and turned to light as they are exposed to the brightness of Love.

MARCH 23rd – BLESS - I am blessing the world. Today, let us focus on being a blessing to the world. Minds connected, thoughts spilling from one to another, mood contagion, all of these lead to blessings. Those same conditions also are the reasons for disturbance. When we project guilt or anger we infect our brothers and sisters. We color the world with fear. When we extend love we see love coming back and minds that are connected also experience love. Everything we express is shared. When we can forgive regret our true selves are revealed to us. As we forgive the shortcomings of others we see them as they are, just like us, pure and loving spirit. So this is the blessing we receive by giving it; we shine our light into the shadows and they dissipate into the truth that is revealed to all.

MARCH 24th – FUNCTIONAL - I am functional. ACIM tells us that our happiness and our function are the same thing. So if we are functioning as we are designed then we are happy. If our function is to bring love to a world bereft. Forgiveness is our function and no matter how disturbing things appear, seeing them healed is still our purpose. Healing starts by accessing the Holy Spirit, accepting His loving thoughts, and then perhaps moving physically into service in the material world. Most important we must see it in our mind, feel it in our heart... As we move through our day there will be temptations to change focus, let us choose to stay the course. Remember that there is no real justification for substituting some other goal. Whatever seems to occur cannot steal our happiness from us if we remember to follow through on our function. It is the function itself that results in happiness.

MARCH 25<sup>th</sup> – LIKENESS - I am in the likeness of Love. We are created in the likeness of our Creator. God is love and created us like love. God is not a body, we are not bodies…God is Spirit, Light and Love…and so are we. Spirit cannot suffer, light cannot lose, love cannot die; these are the attributes of God and likewise of his children. Therefore any suffering that seems to occur cannot be real. The grievances that we hold are the cause of our illusions. These illusions cannot change the truth of who we really are but they can distract us. No situation in the material world concerning a body has anything to do with our true identity. So, no event gives us reason for upset, no reason to feel attacked, and no reason to attack. In Spirit we cannot be harmed so we have no need to try to do harm. If these upsetting feelings occur we only need to stop and remind ourselves that God created us in His image; that Love, Light and Spirit are always safe.

MARCH 26th – FOCUS - I am focused. Take a moment to think about where you are right now…perhaps you seem to be in a room, which is located in a larger building, situated on a parcel of land, maybe in a city, part of a state, belonging to a country, on the planet Earth which is in a solar system that is a member of the Milky Way galaxy, a tiny contingent of the giant universe…get the picture? You, a body in a room and everything in the room and everywhere else is outside of you. Now, consider this alternative: You are Mind and everything that you think is outside of you is actually within you. Your mind is not in your body; your body is in your mind. The room, the building, the land, the state, the country, the planet, the solar system, the galaxy, the universe…all in your mind and your mind is part of God's mind which is all there really is. Focus on this vision and the pettiness of the small self will fall away, all of the tiny grievances which tempt you to think something dangerous is going on outside of you will be as naught.

MARCH 27th – SAFETY - I am safe. The ego is always presenting a plan, it is always making promises that it cannot or will not keep. The refrain is well known to us: "If you get this or that or the other thing, you will feel better". A prize is offered, a goal suggested, a path laid out...let us remember that this is distraction. The alternate goals of the ego obstruct us reaching our true goal. Actually we already have everything that we need and the desires of the ego just keep us from noticing. We are already safe, at home in heaven in God. Hold that thought in mind for a moment: at home, in heaven, in God. Our only worthy goal is to fully remember that place in God that is ours. Other goals distract us, holding grievances further hinders us...today let us choose to see the truth, that only God's plan (our forgiveness) will get us to our ultimate goal.

MARCH 28th – WILL - I am exercising the power of will. There is will and then there is Will. The will of the small self is the voice for separation, it is self-centeredness, it is the one problem, but it is also very small indeed. God's will is our own true will for us. God's will is for good, for the best…the best for us, the best for everyone the best for all of creation. It is also the only true will that exists. Of course, in the material world, we have the power to choose between Goodwill and self-will; and that power of choice is our will. Today let us exercise our will…let us align our will with Goodwill. Let us will that the light of love fill our minds and extend to touch other minds. Let us will that all grievances be healed. Our will aligned with God's will restores us to sanity, restores us to health and wholeness and peace.

MARCH 29th – LIGHT - I am in the light. Light will come to the world when we see that Light is in us. Light will illumine all that we see when we can find it in our brothers and sisters. The light is here now; we do not have to wait any longer. If, today, darkness is seen let us look instead to the Love of God that it might illumine our lives. If shadows are observed in our fellows, let us affirm that those are just the remnants of a dream and then see through to the light. This is God's law, in which only Love exists. There is nothing that can stand against that law simply because there is nothing else. Any opinions to the contrary, even though they seem to be backed by the evidence of the material world, are in error. God's law is "let there be light". And so it is.

MARCH 30th – MIRACULOUS - I am involved in miracles. Many choices will present themselves today. There will probably be challenges and seeming problems. There may appear to be conflict, even ugly brutality in the world we see. We can decide for something else…we can decide for love. We can see through whatever trouble, clear through it, to the light of Love that stands behind all. Let us choose miracles rather than discord. As children of God we have the right to Love, Light, Peace, and Happiness. It is our decision what we will accept…we can stop and live with the illusion of ill or we can involve ourselves with miracles and forgive false appearances.

MARCH 31st – SOLVED - I am solving problems. Today we remember that regardless of the appearance of multiple problems, that we really have only one…one problem… and that problem is self-centeredness. Separation, isolation, uniqueness, disconnection, all the same…self-consciousness, self-pity, self-aggrandizement, self-serving…they are all the same. The descriptions themselves cause an uncomfortable judgment of something that does not even exist. Since we are all connected, we cannot be separate, we can never be isolated…we are one with all Life. The solution to the self (small s) is to find a way to give Love in whatever situation that is causing us to feel apart from life. So a true problem solver will acknowledge a situation and then release ego by asking spirit to reveal what is really there and then follow through on whatever guidance comes.

APRIL 1st – FAITH - I am faithful… What will we have faith in today? Will we put our faith in the darkness of the world or will we have faith in the light of God? It may seem as if there is little choice in this matter, but if we just apply our little bit of willingness we will find that help is available. Liberation from the world is possible right now…just relax and remember that the light in you can change the view from where you seem to stand. Close your eyes, you will not need them. Ask: "What am I?' Soon enough it should become clear that whatever it is that you are it is not a body. If not a body, then what? Somewhere deep within you know that your identity is not physical, but spiritual. Have faith in this, have faith in Spirit because that is what is real…that is what you are.

APRIL 2nd – STRENGTH - I am strong. Quietly now, let us turn our attention from the world to our inner strength. This strength is generated not by the might of the body, but rather by the light of God. This is the strength that makes it possible for us to take responsibility for our lives…to stop being victims of the world that we see. Strength, which does not revel in the small self, but finds true expression in the Greater. Consider it now, true strength created in Light and generator of light. Accept it, feel it, then notice how it heals inner hurts and can be used to shine on outer circumstances…watch as this brightness washes over the shadows dissipating them and leaving naught but love in its wake. Rejoice, because today something much greater than the small self is beginning to be revealed. Throughout the day think often of this vast inner reservoir and tap into as often as you will.

APRIL 3rd – INSIDE - I am on the inside. It is easy to believe that we are bodies existing in a world filled with other bodies that are in competition with us for limited resources. This thought system of lack is the ego's main defensive. We identity ourselves with what we do in the world, we identify others according to what we think they do in the world. We have believed that we are our behaviors. Take a moment to recognize that we are not in the world, we are not our deeds, and that we are not bodies. We are part of God, we are on the inside and there is no outside. We are inside of God; and Light, Love, Peace and Joy are inside of us. Focusing on what is on the inside we will surely change how we perceive the outside.

APRIL 4th – REMAIN - I am as I am. We may believe that we have done many things, which increased or decreased our worth. Yet our worth has never really fluctuated. The ego continues to count deeds and misdeeds in a cipher that will never balance out. As we have heard many times we are "Created in the image and likeness of God." God does not change, so our true Self does not change. We remain as created. We are as we are…we do not make but yet create… we remain in our true place but still extend…we are as we are. All past mistakes can be corrected and healed just by this remembrance. To remember that Love remains and that we remain with Love, that is the balm. To know that we have no power to change what God has created gives us all the power to change the suffering that we have made.

APRIL 5th – ONE - I am one Self. We continue working with the most important theme in our study…we are and always will be One. We are unified with all Life. Our experience in the world continues to deny this. The ego is always looking for ways to point out the duality of existence…that there is good and there is evil. This is the view symbolized in the creation story relating Eve's run in with the serpent and the whole affair with the apple. It is this view; this thought system that has made the world that we see. A world of threat and danger, a world of blood and death is the ego's playground. In the midst of this horror there is safety. That safety lies in our ability to see through the illusion of division to the truth of unity. Safety comes from Spirit, which is our one true Self. When we think with Spirit, as Spirit, we come to peace.

APRIL 6th – ONE - I am undivided. We have been experiencing life as two entities. Our self seems to be split between mind and body...we are divided within ourselves and therefore we have conflict, this conflict shows itself in the world, Mind trying to control body but not entirely successful. Mind trying to find self-expression through the body, but we are not bodies. We are spirit...spirit expresses through mind. We are safe in our true Self...we are safe in Spirit. Today we get quiet and relax back into a peaceful state...we still the crying of the small self and allow the voice for God speak. Here, at peace, in love we are home...safe... sound...undivided. The conflict of the world fades away because we are healing the rift in our own mind.

APRIL 7th – SPIRIT - I am spirit. Today we will attempt to release body identification. We reject the divided life we have lived and accept our true identity. Being spirit means that we were born of spirit, in that we are of God. In reality we are divine. None of the limits of the world apply here. All disease, disorder, and dysfunction are healed. There is no danger that can threaten. We are united with all life, united with all those we have ever known and all those we have yet to meet. From the perspective of spirit we see that we are totally unbound from all past misperceptions and future fears. In Spirit we can change the way see the world... we can view it from the eyes of love and set it free...that will actually change the way it is.

APRIL 8th – PLAN - I am a part of God's plan. God does not really plan, God simply wills, and it is so. We, however, have thought that we can oppose God's will. This erroneous thinking accounts for all the guilt that is present in the ego. All part of the illusion, our "sins" are tools that the ego uses to keep the idea of separation viable. Our mistakes are but wisps of fog that will disappear in the Light. The instant we decided to go it alone, God provided the way back to Unity... that is God's plan. Wholeness accomplished in that same moment when the separation happened and it is available to us right now. We just need to accept it...God will not force happiness upon us. Nevertheless the way is open to us through our own forgiveness and that is God's plan...that we forgive the world and return to the Love we never really left.

APRIL 9th – ROLE - I am fulfilling my role. In the material world we seem to have many roles. We may have taken on career, family, financial, athletic, spiritual, educational, sexual and hobby roles. Regardless of the role we play we still have only one function and that is to be truly helpful. This function has been described as our life mission, our purpose for being, and even as the way to the fulfillment of our destiny. This purpose is compassionate, understanding, loving…it is the embodiment of forgiveness. So whatever our activity in the world our main effort is to forgive all of the perceived ugliness, to forgive all of the fear, hate, anger, anxiety, upset, sickness, deprivation…all of it. To be the light of the world, shining away all of the false evidence of separation. This work seems to be difficult only when we believe that we have to do it alone; but we are not alone. In order for us to accomplish our one true task we need only ask the Spirit within, our one true Self, to show us what to do. We just go about our normal days performing all of our material world tasks in our material world roles with just one difference, we listen to guidance as to what to do in each moment and situation. Then, we will be automatically fulfilling our one true function, plus all of the rest.

APRIL 10th – UNFOLDING - I am unfolding my good. Remembering that we have a function and that that function is also our happiness can be motivating in moments when we find ourselves holding back. We unfold our good as we move into alignment with goodwill. The world we see is our world to change, and it cannot be changed by outer activities alone. We are really the only ones who can change the world we see, so that means no one else is going to do it. It will continue to change for the worst in an automatic way according to how we designed it, but if we really want to heal the hate, it must be by our spiritual efforts. Going forth on one crusade or another, fighting against the perceived evils of the world will not affect true change even if we are successful in one area. True change will come when we start on the inside, getting quiet. Forgiving all of our brothers and sisters (and ourselves) …seeing the whole thing differently and then going about our normal business. The business of living and loving in the present moment, and giving ourselves spontaneously to the world. Our good will continue to unfold and it will be Good for all.

APRIL 11th – JOY - I am joyful. When we recognize that Goodwill is good for all, we will start to understand that Creation is not upset with us; it is not holding our mistakes against us. God, the universe, Creation, whatever you want to call it is not judging us...we are judging us. We have believed that we are on our own, that we left God, that we have consciously fought against Him, and that He must be upset about it. All of these things are just part of the illusion. We are just having a bad dream in which we are sometimes acting badly...it is not real. God's will, cannot be overturned by a weak dream. God's will is for good. God's will is for Unity. God's will is for Love. God cannot be separated from His will and neither can we. So, for the rest of the day, remind yourself that sin is not real, it is just an illusion...it never happened in reality. Remember also that Peace and Joy and Happiness are the gifts of God that have been given us by birthright. They are God's will and that cannot be changed.

APRIL 12th – SHARE - I am sharing God's will. Ok, so we are starting to at least consider the idea that God is happy with us and wants us to be happy. Unfortunately we will still slip back into guilt and shame. Ego believes that the only way to maintain its existence is to block awareness of the true love of God, which is radiating within, between and all around us. This blocking is accomplished through continually reminding us of past misperceptions and giving us anxious thoughts about the future. Regret and resentments and fear of an uncertain future keep us from living in the moment. Not living in the moment is really not living at all. Quietly now, without making a fuss, just gently release the past and the future into God's hands. Give it all into His care. The Holy Spirit loves to receive our problems and turn them back into gifts…because it is His will that we be whole with Him. Happy, healthy and free…sounds good doesn't it? This is God's eternal offer to us. Why not accept it? Our true desire cannot be different than the Will of He who created us.

APRIL 13th – TEACHER – I am teaching happiness. We are all teaching, all the time. We teach lessons of fear or we teach benefits of love. We can teach happiness by being happy. We can teach non-judgment by not judging. It is neither important nor helpful to call people's apparent shortcomings to their attention. It is however quite beneficial to recognize the good in others and teach them that. We can be happy finding the good in all. In this way all are raised higher in consciousness. We can decide today what we will reinforce...truth or lies. Let us teach only love, giving that which is called for in all situations. As we offer this example, we are ministers of God and teachers of happiness.

APRIL 14th – REALITY – I am seeking my real Self. Let us seek what is ours in reality. We are in reality when we can observe the unity of all life. We are real in the light of Good. Today let us release the illusion that the apparent behavior of others determines our wellbeing. We can let go of the hate that we harbor. Examine the reality…there is no reason to expect anyone to act the way we think we need them to act. First it relegates them to a role and makes them an object. Second it ties our happiness to the actions of the figments of our imagination. This is the truth, when we believe that others are either a threat to us or our protection against the dangers of the world they are not real, they are just shadows we have created in the darkness of self-centeredness. Be real; be reconciled with life.

APRIL 15th – UNION – I am unified. Let us offer unity to each one we meet. Unity and equality are the gifts of the day. Holding onto levels of relationships keeps us all in bondage. It may seem natural to have stronger feelings for some people in our lives than for some others. These strong feelings can appear to be either good or bad. We have good feelings for those we think are closer to us. We have bad feelings for those who we discern are a threat to us. We hold those around us hostage to our own delusional whims. We will do well to recognize the only difference in these relationships is how we perceive the past behavior of each person. Given time we will move them from one category to another, and we probably are entertaining multiple categories. This is the division of relationship and it is false. The truth is we are unified, we are a part of all and all are a part of us.

APRIL 16th – Quiet – I am quiet. Becoming still we know the truth... We are complete…but sometimes we are feeling much less than this. Heaven is our goal and in fact we have already attained it…we have only dreamed that we have left it. Our practice now is to quietly come back into awareness. We really do not have to do anything but surrender to the presence of Spirit within us. If we find our thoughts straying to conflict, let us be willing to let Spirit cleanse us. The tiniest portion of willingness on our part will link to the great power that is always present in us. We will see our completeness and then will be comforted and at ease. So, today, let us just relax into peace of mind and allow that Mind to guide us to oneness.

APRIL 17th – FORGIVE – I am forgiving. Forgiveness leads to the Truth. Forgiveness is letting go of the past. Letting go of the past frees us from all conflict. It is only by focusing on the past that we can hold on to misery. In the present, in the Holy Moment there is naught but bliss. Love lives in and through us in eternity, it cannot exist in our thoughts when we are attracted to a past occurrence or when we are projecting into an uncertain future. Forgiveness happens when we forget past hurts, when we choose love instead of fear. Anger flees in the face of God's goodness. The light of Creation dissipates the shadows of fragmentation. As we forgive we are healed and we heal all of those whom we have held in the bondage of guilt and shame. Let us release these nightmarish demons right now and come into harmony with all of our brothers and sisters. Let us see the truth.

APRIL 18th – WILLING – I am willing to give. The beginning of willingness is the opening for Truth to enter. The truth of giving is that we cannot lose. We cannot give what we do not have and we cannot lose what we have by giving it. In the material world this seems incorrect. We disprove this by relying on Spirit to make proper gifts. We can be so attached to the material world that it is difficult to let go. All of our life experiences are potential for distraction. Holding on to false evidence hinders us in our search. If we ask for guidance it will be delivered. Stop trying to do anything on your own. Nothing real is accomplished out of the personality…alone we can do nothing. Literally all of our reactions to the events of the day are nothing but continued attempts to see lack in a universe of abundance. Today, let us align our will with Goodwill…let us decide to give with God's guidance.

APRIL 19<sup>th</sup> – REST – I am resting. The Holy Spirit is charged with transforming our perceptions. Sometimes it seems that there is no rest. The great transformer is in us, and always operating for our benefit. He offers light for darkness. He offers peace for conflict. He offers rest for weariness. A path out of this exhausting life of fear and anger is available to us at every moment of every day. Just relax, release, and let go. Ease into the company of your brothers, relax into Spirit, and rest within God. Be open to the gifts that are present for you and release any expectations. Forgive the past and let go of any worry for the future. Resting is really just remembering peace. Let us attempt to recall the truth…the real world is here and it is now...just obscured by the shadows. The healing light of God is calming us right now...Let us turn our attention to that comfort.

APRIL 20th – RESURRECTION – I am restored to sanity. We are resurrected in the light of God. We are brought back to our original state... we are saved from a life of suffering. Salvation has become such a charged word; all sorts of strange religious connotations abound in regards to it. Some very weird ideas have come forth in relation to it. Salvation is a natural miracle. Salvation literally means health and wholeness. It cannot be purchased because it is already ours. It cannot be taken from us because it is integral to who we are and cannot be divided from us. It also cannot be realized alone. The miracle of salvation is a group activity so to speak. We cannot experience it alone. This means the idea of personal salvation is erroneous; salvus comes from oneness. When the many become One we are saved. No one can be left behind. When we are reconciled with our fellows we rely on our shared strength and we then find that all are healed.

APRIL 21st – CREATED – I am the light that God created. Today we will attempt to come out of the shadows. Let us remember that we can only be as we were created. We can let go of every other seeming attribute. We can forgive who we seem to be in order to come into direct contact with what we really are. We are Son of God...all of us together are Son of God. Every time we meet someone we have an opportunity to unify our Self. People we think we know present our past experiences to us, people we think we don't know show us dark future possibilities. Of course, both are the same, just seen from different perspectives...both are wraiths...shadows drawn over our true identity. It is our ego that generates the shadows...little replicas of itself which it then projects onto others. Take a moment now and allow the light that shines within to come forth. Notice how the light in you dissipates the shadows you have gathered around yourself. This cleanses our brothers and us...restoring us to our true Self...the light and love that God created.

APRIL 22nd – CLEAR – I am clear. Today we look past circumstances and see the truth. We allow ourselves to be transparent so that the light of joy shines through us, delivering peace to all. Holy Spirit is continually trying to return us to happiness in the kingdom of Heaven. Spirit's purpose is simple, strip away all of the lies we have told ourselves and reveal the reality beyond our perception. To link our purpose to the Teacher's purpose is to hurry our happy return Home. So let us be clear in our intentions, we intend to remember who we really are. We return to the divine by giving the light of creation (which is what we are) to everyone we meet. Things happen and then we try to figure out what it meant…and we are generally wrong. Begin with the end in mind. We want to be who we really are. Every situation we find ourselves in can be an opportunity to practice our purpose and find our Identity. If we hold our goal of unity in mind, we can accomplish it moment by moment.

APRIL 23rd – FAITH – I am faithful. Today, let us stop accepting substitutes for what we really want. Faith is our perceiving faculty. It is our ability to see past the apparent details of our suffering and know the truth. Here is the reality, at home and at peace, we are one Self, part of life and as such part of God. Every apparent situation in the world that we have made is relational. All of life is about relationships, relationships with other people and ideas. Life in the material world is all just one thing after another…one distraction after another…we are missing the truth because we are using these distractions to keep us from uncovering the highest reality: Unity. This is where faith comes in; to change the way we perceive…using the Light of our true self to see through the darkness all the way to safety.

APRIL 24th – SON – I am a child of God. We are not bodies caught in time; we are eternal Spirit. The instant is eternity. Creation exists only in the present; we exist only in the present. The past is gone, the future never will be. Today, let us commit to bringing our attention to our present moment. The more intention we put into keeping our focus in the moment the closer we come to the holy instant. In the Holy instant we experience safety. We are released from depression, sickness, pain and darkness... that is the function of the moment. To actually live in the present means that we are free from the past. In the moment we can be our true selves, we have no reason to attack, we have no problems that plague, we have no worries or fears. In the moment we are God's children, whole and free... in the moment we are together and therefore we are saved.

APRIL 25th – ROLE -- I am unconditional. Today, we can re-establish our true role. We can take on the responsibility of service. We can release people from the roles and categories we have put them in, taking back our own role. Being confused, and thinking that people are provided for our own gratification is not helpful. We must closely examine our tendency to assign roles to our brothers and sisters. Every relationship that we have can lend itself to this sort of control and projection. If we desire peace, we will stop judging one against another. We will begin to see that we are all of equal value and that our value lies in our true identity, not in what we do or don't do. We are all connected in the vast web of life and each of us has a true task to accomplish, let us get out of the way so our brother may accomplish his work and that we may do likewise. To give unconditional, proper service to others is the highest aspiration that we can hold. Let us release any other goal. Give all to have all. No more comparing, see only equality and unity…let us be unconditional.

APRIL 26th – DREAM – I am waking to happiness. Let us attempt a small awakening today. In the past we may have thought it pleasant to live in a fantasy world where magic acts to bring about our wishes and desires. At first look this seems desirable, a paradise…but looking more closely we find that our fantasies generally involve anger, revenge, and the control of others. Consider the news of the day… whatever disasters we watch unravel, we have conflicting opinions about what should be done. We feel powerless to do anything, so we begin to fantasize about punishment for those involved. We may see some utopian vision of how the world could be if our values were somehow foisted upon everyone else. Let us stop this self-aggrandized dream. Let go the hostages of our dark vision and see the situation in the light of God. Give it to Spirit to correct our seeing and that will allow true happiness to come forth, in us and in all others.

APRIL 27th – RECEIVING --- I am receiving. We are receiving the joy of God right now. We can be at peace knowing that we are cared for in every moment. The Creator is moving in and through us as joy and peace. We need have no fear of lack, so we can be free in our giving. We give to life and life gives to us. We are the Power of happiness expressing as us in life. We can carry our own weight, doing the things that need to be done by us, but we are unafraid to ask for help when we need it. We give as we receive, and we receive as we give. In this way we become part of the great flow of good in the universe. As we share freely without concern, we are provided for without effort. What may, at first, appear to be difficult is easily accomplished by us when we act from our joy. However, we also have learned to give wisely from inner guidance. Sometimes we must restrain our generosity if it appears that our help may actually allow someone to become stuck in dependence. We would do better to teach interdependence. Let us trust the joy of God to direct us in our giving, knowing that the same happiness is directing even more peace our way.

APRIL 28th – HEART --- I am loving. We can rest in the Truth, and that truth will wash away all illusions. We know that we can only give what we have already received and that we can only keep what we receive by sharing it freely. God lives in the heart as the Supreme Giver – she leads our true Self, restores our youthful outlook, refreshes our generosity, fires our love, illuminates our wisdom. She dispels any seeming darkness or evil and she guards our love and our loved ones. This urge to give freely comes straight from the Divine in our heart. There may have been times when fear cautioned us to hold tight to things, today we release all such thoughts. We know that we are richly blessed and so we can give from the heart. As we move through our day, we take courage, we are full of energy and we will notice many opportunities to give. We can be generous and allow the Good in us to express in whatever way we are guided. We are filled with the love and light of God.

APRIL 29th – REST --- I am resting. I can relax and trust God to care for my loved ones and me. I allow my mind to become one with the mind of God. This is a quality of being, a field of goodwill that extends from me to those whom I am praying for. I know that when I pray for my loved ones not only do they benefit but so am I and all of those around me. I set up a positive vibration that radiates out in all directions. This is the very love of God, which cares for me, my loved ones and even those who I may not at this time consider loved. I trust this power to see to the well being of family and friends. I do not have to interfere in the lives of others. This presence and power of Creation is working in and through everyone. So I can trust God to care for my loved ones. I know that I am created in the likeness of God and that so are my brothers and sisters...so I can be myself and I can allow them to be as they are also.

APRIL 30th – LOVE – I am in love. We are in love, of love and all love. Love cannot be learned it is part of our make up. Love cannot be acquired through some action; it is freely given and then abundantly received. Our relationship with our fellows is rooted in this love...it is our ultimate connection to all that lives. However, we have been experiencing something quite different. When our lives seem to be in conflict...when we feel at odds with our brothers or just the world in general we have strayed from love. We are directly responsible for our own experience of life. Let us decide for love, to be in love...this is our heritage and our function. Our function is love...this shows itself in our experience. In the world we give love as forgiveness. In heaven (oneness) we give love as extension (creation). This is our true state, to be in love. Relish it.

MAY 1st – HAPPINESS --- I am happy. Happiness comes from seeing things in the light of love which will in turn change our minds concerning the nature of life. Life seems short as we watch the body age. Sometimes I may worry that as time goes on I will lose my ability to live life fully. I may believe that my faculties will diminish and I will slow down. I am determined to change my mind in this regard. I am the image and likeness of God, I am filled with the life of God, I am part of the life that never ends. My essence exists in eternity, which cannot be divided in past, present and future…it is the eternal now. I am determined to remain youthful in mind and body. And even if my body does not fully cooperate, I still keep my outlook positive. I am committed to continue to learn and to grow. I am first and foremost a spirit and that will remain a constant. I am part of eternal life and that is rich indeed!

MAY 2nd – IMAGE -- I am making the world that I see. We can forgive the world. If we see an image of prosperity, that is what we will experience. If we see an image of lack, that is what we will get. When we forgive lack we see correctly. When we think of prosperity, what does that look like? We can imagine perfect prosperity. Whatever the image is, we can make it so! We can forgive the world by forming mental pictures of a perfect, loving and abundant place, God's perfect world. We can clearly see all people and ourselves around the world living in abundance...living in peace and harmony with everyone. We see the planet healed. We have the ability to envision a garden where we may have seen destruction. We see others and ourselves as caretakers of the world. We are careful with the Earth. We are privileged to conserve energy and resources. We forgive the separation and image all things unified, knowing this can become our reality, and we hold to these visions with faith.

MAY 3rd – GRATEFUL – I am grateful. Let us be grateful for the gifts of God. We have been given all of the power we need to forgive the world of death and destruction. We can return to the love of God any time we choose. We are able use our thoughts to create a new reality. We have a vision of wholeness for everyone. We can see an abundance of good for the entire world. We know that we can help this vision become reality. As I sit quietly, I feel my heart filling with God's gift of love. When it is filled to overflow, I extend this stream of love out into the world. I see my family and friends receiving this love as a continuous stream of light. I am just the facilitator, I trust God to give them their own vision and show them how to express their own gifts. I expand my vision to see this light moving over my community, blessing and awakening all of those whom it touches. My vision grows still larger as the light extends across the country, healing divisions as it does. The light encircles the planet bringing peace and harmony to the whole world.

MAY 4th – FOREVER -- I am forever. Everybody dies; this may seem a bleak prospect but only to bodies. Every body dies, but we are not bodies. Our bodies are constructs, generated out of the design of the super ego. Our separated mind projecting a material world in which our material bodies compete for material stuff keeps us locked into the illusion of limited life. Life is actually unlimited and we are an integral part of it. We are not bodies, we are spirit. The experience of life in spirit is totally different than life in the body; we cannot be sure of what the experience actually is but we are assured in ACIM that it is greater than our present imagination can conceive. So being in eternity, being a part of eternal life means trading our self-consciousness for God consciousness. That sounds like a good trade.

MAY 5th – IMAGE -- I am receiving. I am gifted with images from Spirit. As I get quiet I receive an image of prosperity. When I think of prosperity, what does that look like? I can imagine perfect prosperity. Whatever my image is, I can make it so! I form mental pictures of the real world, a loving and abundant place, and God's perfect world. I can clearly see all people and myself around the world living in abundance. I see us living in peace and harmony with everyone. I see the planet healed. I have the ability to envision a garden where I may have seen destruction. I see others and myself as caretakers of the world. We are careful with the Earth. We are privileged to conserve energy and resources. I image all of these things, knowing they can become reality, and I hold to these visions with faith.

MAY 6th – GIFT – I am giving and receiving. Today I give of myself and I receive the good of God. I give my gift of divine vision. I use my divine vision to co-create with God. I am able to use my thoughts to create a new reality. I have a vision of prosperity for everyone. In prayer I see an abundance of good for the entire world. I know that I can help this vision become reality by giving to it. As I sit quietly, I feel my heart fill with love. When it is filled to overflow, I extend this love to the world. I see my family and friends receiving this love as a continuous stream of light. I am just the facilitator, I trust God to give them their own vision and show them how to express their own gifts. I expand my vision to see this light moving over my community, blessing and awakening all of those whom it touches. My vision grows still larger as the light extends across the country, healing divisions as it does. The light encircles the planet bringing peace and harmony to the whole world. This peace and harmony becomes firmly fixed in my mind and truly becomes mine as I give it.

MAY 7th – LOVE -- I am loved. The love of God is true abundance; it is not limited by any other circumstance. I will not achieve true prosperity without exploring the love that is flowing to me right now. We all have a part to play and place to be in creation. So I can be confident that I am an integral part of Love and my purpose is the working of that part. All of this love is really one Love: God's Love. As part of that Oneness I see that it is my purpose to extend love and forgiveness to all whom I meet. I give love as I share my gifts with others, and as a result I receive many gifts in return. So, today I will be purposeful in all that I do. Prosperity and plenty come to me as a direct result of me acting in the world with purpose. I have a place in God that no one else can fill…I have a combination of talents and abilities that are given to me in trust. My purpose is to lovingly polish and hone these gifts…and then to give them away.

MAY 8th – VALUE -- I am re-evaluating. That which I have previously valued has clouded my vision. The kingdom of Heaven is my true goal...it is not some far off place to be found after death, but rather a state of mind to be realized now. My mission is a daily application of my purposeful journey to that state of mind. As the day unfolds, I look for ways to be truly helpful, ignoring the urging of ego. My mission always is to be helpful at every opportunity. As I greet the new day I do so with a view toward service. I lovingly contribute to my household, to the neighborhood, to the community, and to world.... trying to establish a pure vision of God's love in action. Every temptation to accept some lesser goal I will pass over in favor of the Greater.

MAY 9<sup>th</sup> – DIRECTION -- I am directed beyond this world. I put my attention where I want to go. I have learned the secret of direction. What I focus on grows, where I put my vision is the path that my feet will follow. I am single minded in my pursuit of mission and purpose. By focusing on what I want to accomplish, the way is made for me to achieve and succeed. My vision points me to Unity. Today let our path move us in the direction of Heaven (the kingdom of oneness). Once we have surrendered to the still, small voice within we will surely be guided correctly.

MAY 10th – CORRECTION -- I am correcting my course. Whereas I have been seeing double, I now see One. My double vision, seeing both good and bad has confused me. In Spirit there is only good. This good cannot be correctly perceived as something that occurs only in part. God's will is for Good and therefore that is all there is. God's will is for abundance. We are connected…that is God's will. We are all a part of the great fabric of life. Love is our heritage because we are one with it. There is no lack; there is no evil! Many times we may have wished and hoped for some good thing to come us. We may have prayed, begging or even demanding that God deliver the good(s). Today, we can have a single vision, knowing that we are connected to all of the Good that the universe has for us. It is not something we have to long for; the peace of God is just something we have to accept. This connection to all Good is our link to all of the good that we need. Our correct course lies in allowing the good that God has given us to flow through us.

MAY 11th –HEALING - I am healing. Today, we find what we seek by sincerely asking for it. Just a little willingness will suffice. We can heal all conflict by having faith, faith in our brother and faith in God. Every event seen rightly is a divine opportunity for enlightenment. Truth needs no healing; it is only the vagaries of small mind that cause us to think we are sick. Health and wholeness in all of our affairs relies on seeing true purpose and allowing divine mind to use us for that purpose. Our purpose (our goal and our happiness) is to find the Good in life and in our fellows. We are healed and we are healers in direct proportion to our faith. Not faith in a superstitious way but rather in the sense of perceiving the truth of God in all living things…to see the Christ in our neighbor…to notice good all around. Acceptance of oneness is what we seek and that will accomplish the healing of all ills. Unity is our balm and our medicine, harmony is the cure and indeed the healing itself.

MAY 12th – RELEASE - I am letting go of opinions. We have many opinions concerning the world, these opinions actually block peace. Let us examine the barriers to peace so that we can erase them from our thinking. Some of these will come quite clearly from our own twisted desire for chaos…. some will seem to be someone else's fault. Our brothers will appear to be uncooperative and the events of the day will conspire to steal our joy. When we let go of our self-centered view of the world we find quiet and miraculously the world calms down. Peace can and will overcome all of these projections. Peace will not beat them into submission, but rather it will embrace every conflict with love and render it like unto itself. From peace we carry a message of love, we are yoked in light with our brothers, ever extending our Fathers kingdom. Happiness and total calm is available to us right now…it already lives deep within us, waiting for our willingness to allow it to come forth.

MAY 13th – PRIORITY - I am changing priorities. We have chosen disorder over divine order. We have assigned worth to the worthless and denigrated that which is precious. We made idols out of the desires of the ego. Today let us choose what is Good and what is True. When we recognize that everything is in divine order the peace of God is ours and we can see what is really important. The problem is that much of the time we desire chaos and conflict. We live in the middle of bliss and yet we put our attention on substitutes that cannot possibly replace it. We are the architects of our own adversity…thinking it be excitement we seek danger and madness. Happily, Spirit lives deep within us and it is always ready to clear away the conflict and show us the truth of our being. All things work together for good, for those who love. Peace flows across whatever obstacle the ego may put in the way, no matter how unfortunate the events of the day seem to be, peace flows across to establish itself as the answer. Today, let us call it forth, releasing our attraction for drama in favor of everlasting love.

MAY 14th – SINLESS – I am innocent. We are all innocent. Let us see differently. Innocence means unaware of sinful things. Our brothers are innocent, we are innocent, and we are all innocent. Forgiveness is a release from judgment, a return to innocence. All throughout this day let us stop comparing our sins; let us release any sense of judgment. "Judge not, that ye be not judged." It means exactly what it says… all judgment comes from us. We can only place a negative judgment on our brother by placing one on ourselves. We have crucified ourselves upon the frame of our perceived sins and we continually call our brother to climb up there with us. Misery's company is a poor substitute for the oneness that is available through forgiveness. Today, let us affirm that we are all sinless. Let us redeem ourselves through the redemption of all those who we have called to judgment. Release the hostages, let them go and be free. Have faith, have faith in our brother, and have faith in God. Let us embrace our shared perfection and be innocent.

MAY 15th – DEFENSELESS – I am defenseless. Since, in Truth, we cannot be attacked we need no defense. In the world we seem to always be under attack...this is only because we are always attacking. Defensive action is a symbol of our irrational fear of God. Long now, we have been afraid of God. Leaving God, fighting against God, usurping God's role seem to be our great sins...surely these are unforgivable. Let us be clear today, we cannot leave God, we cannot turn our back on God, we cannot go anywhere where God is not, and we cannot be and never have been apart from God. There is no death, so nothing to fear, there is no judgment, so nothing to regret, and there is no payment to be extracted so there is no retribution to fear. The ego fears...it fears for its existence, but we are not our egos. We are of God, in God and integral to God. Our father has nothing but Good for us, which can replace the seeming evil in the world. He and all the wonders of creation await us just beyond the veil of shadows that we have erroneously woven out of our fear. Today, we make an attempt to let down the defenses and let the light shine in.

MAY 16th – HEALED - I am healing. All of our sickness is but a symptom of our attempt to separate from God. In our separate weirdness, we have designed ourselves to get sick. Sickness reminds us of our feigned weakness. This happens at a subconscious level and so feeling guilty about it is silly and just adds to the pain that we DON'T have to endure. Life in the body lends itself to suffering and illness. Life in spirit is painless because we embrace the Love of Heaven. Contrary to common wisdom we have nothing to fear from the apparent breakdowns of the body…this may be hard to accept but are nonetheless real. The body has one proper function. This function is the communication of forgiveness. We have gotten it mixed up. We have come to believe that the body contains our life, but our life is contained in God. We are focused on the thing, which divides us. Expecting the body to heal the separation, which it is a creation of, is a vanity. Today, we release guilt and projection and allow healing to flow from within alleviating all sickness.

MAY 17th – JOIN - I am joined with my brother. We are filled with life and that life is whole and perfect. We have been tempted to accept sickness and eventual death…thinking martyrdom attractive in some strange way. Singularly unattractive, this insane idea springs from the ego, which has made sin and guilt and sickness and death seem inevitable. This is in direct contravention of the laws of God…therefore it cannot be true. God's will is for life and for the continual expansion of life. We are part of the incorruptible body of Christ. When we accept that we are healed, we also facilitate healing in our brother, because we are joined. Even a small bit of cooperation with the healing process will yield out of proportion results for all of our fellows and us. Our bodies are symbols and not something that we use as a way to connect us with God; our true, immortal Self is always connected. We do not need symbols to make this real…we are continually in communion with our brothers and with God…this is the eternal truth of our existence. We are joined and in that joining all things are shared.

MAY 18th – DECIDE – I am deciding for the light. Today, we decide in favor of the light. It is a decision to hear the song of Creation…a decision to see Heaven. Creation sings a song; it is the song of light. Sound and sight combine in this infinite dance of love. All safety lies in our choice to dance this dance of life. We cannot be harmed in any undertaking, which moves us into the extension of that which we truly are. Pain is a useless lesson. Our present world is designed to teach through pain. Even when we believe we are victorious we are actually defeated. It is only through the release of all individual (self-centered) goals that we can find the real world and the peace that entails. This does not mean that we resign ourselves to a meager existence; rather it is our greatest calling…to remember that alone we can do nothing and so to attempt nothing alone. All goals should be of spirit and in cooperation with life. Remembering the light means to "Seek first the kingdom…", doing so we will find that true abundance is always ours.

MAY 19th – ACCEPTANCE – I am accepting Unity. We are coming to an understanding of how this world works. We are totally responsible for what we see; we can see One or many. We can see fear or love. It is totally up to us. This may seem to be a difficult acceptance…it does not matter…it is the truth. We choose the feelings that we feel…we decide upon the goal we put our attention on…all the things that seem to happen are only those things, which we have asked for. This then is the day when we decide to ask for what we really want. Atonement is actually the release of suffering and sin. It is the entrance into instant happiness and the accomplishment of the one true goal. Today, let us accept our true state. When we do this our happiness grows and it becomes our gift to ourselves and to all of our brothers. Our perception changes from conflict to harmony…from hell to heaven…and we are then responsible for paradise.

MAY 20th – CURE – I am cured. With faith in the safety of God we are cured (made whole). Faith is the perception we invest in our life events…belief is the story we tell ourselves that confirms our faith…vision is the world we see as a result. We already have all the faith, belief and vision that are needed to enter into the Kingdom of heaven. Where we have been using our faith to confirm the danger of the world, we can now change the application. The Holy Spirit will show us the way home if we but ask. The way will be made clear for us. Perception will change as we work with the Voice for God, as our belief system is changed. Vision will be restored as the shadows of fear are wiped from our eyes. Endeavor throughout the day to apply the cure (salvation): have faith in yourself, in your brother and in God. Remember that these three are really all one and the same. Faith is the medium in which belief leads to the vision of Heaven… remember that.

MAY 21st – FORGIVE – I am forgiving. Today, let us release all fear to the miracle of forgiveness. Sometimes we may think that if we look too closely within ourselves that we will find some horror that we cannot bear. It seems easier to look without. Our happiness is lost as we look without and see all of our projected fears reflected back at us in the form of judgment…we judge our brothers as being outside of grace and generally lacking in that which today we believe they should have. We may judge harshly, seeing behavior, which is anathema to us. We may judge more positively having a sort of compassion as we observe the suffering of others. All of this is just a distraction from the truth. The truth can only be found within. We must dive down below the surface appearances of life, past the veneer of civilization, past the animal responses of ego, through all of the fears and enter directly into the light that is our spirit. This is the core of Goodness that we find in us and then are able to see in our brother. This vision is everything we really want because it releases all of us from the chains of sin and sickness. Today, let us see the truth, forgiving appearance and finding happiness.

MAY 22nd – GIFTS -- I am gifted. Today, let us choose to accept the grace of God. Grace is dedicated to the restoration to sanity. The gifts of God all reflect our inherent Oneness with all life. This ultimate unity is God's will and nothing can oppose it. Grace reconnects our will to Goodwill. Grace will not allow any thought of separation to keep us from the truth because it knows only connectedness. Grace has no weakness or division…it is complete in its ability to see only One. Grace knows only God and sees only God in all things. This is our hope and our cause…to come into this integrated state of mind. Grace allows us to remember that the world we see is a mirror, which reflects our choices back to us. Sometimes it seems that our mirror has broken into a million fragments and that then, insanely these fragments have grown arms and legs to fight with one another. Grace gently corrects this distortion…discarding this mad vision for the sanity of Heaven. Today, it is grace that we choose.

MAY 23rd – CALM – I am calm. Many times we are stressed and we call out for the answer to our troubles. Daily we find challenges and sufferings…we ask why? We can use this time today, to find the answer. First we need to get quiet, become calm and centered. In silence we can hear the still small voice. We will be shown that our only problem is our sense of separation from Creation…this is the sole cause of all of our maladies, all of our pain and suffering. This sense of aloneness is a lie that we have told ourselves. The solution to these troubles are also found in stillness…we realize that all that we give…all that we give to the world and all that we give to spirit we give to ourselves. It is much easier to decide what to do and what to say when we know that whatever it is will be our gift to life and therefore, to ourselves. Let us be calm, let us go within before we go without, and let us remember that all that we do is done to ourselves.

MAY 24th – INCLUSIVE – I am in God. Everyone, everything, all of Creation is inclusively in God. There is literally nothing but God. God is in us…we are in God. In God is the only true joy, the only true peace, the only true love, and the only true life…these are not different, indeed they are one. Our words cannot convey the power of this idea. It is only dimly that we can see the full ramifications of these symbols. An inner shift is needed to move us closer the bridge of spirit which stands ready to erase the imaginary distance between us and our father. Reason and order are always in place…no matter how far we seem to have moved from them…they are there to comfort us when we choose again. Despite the appearance of the world, happiness is always available, peace is constantly present, love is forever extending. The world holds nothing of value for us; it is only in the unity of Spirit that we can find what is precious. Today, let us shift our attention from the outer madness to our inner reality and embrace the light that always shines within us.

MAY 25th – REALITY --- I am strong in the reality of Spirit. The physical world is just a shadow of Reality. Just beneath the surface is the remembrance of Truth. When we open ourselves to the Holy Spirit we begin to see what lies beyond the material world. It is the through this opening that our abundance manifests itself. Things are just symbols; it is up to us how we interpret them. The strength in us is an untapped well of good fortune. Creation has invested us with an overflowing abundance of strength. Be confident in the presence of God. Know that Spirit is continually renewing our ability to deal with whatever may occur. We have the power to reinterpret events...understanding that good is always available. We can relax and let go of any worry. Reality is Good; anything that is not is not real.

MAY 26th – EXPECT --- I am expectant. Today, expect to find the Truth. Worry is a distraction; it is fearful prayer. 'Fear is actually a kind of faith; it is really having faith in fearful things. Whether we are concerned about the outcome of a particular project or event or just generally anxious, we are putting our faith in negative outcomes. We can change our minds any time we wish. Today let us decide to look for and expect right outcomes. Expect to move over and through all the events of the day. Each day will present various issues. Through loving expectation, we can solve each and every problem. We can let go of all preconceived ideas and move forward with open minds into our day.

MAY 27th – WORTH --- I am choosing what I want. Today, let us examine what we really want. We must take responsibility for our choices and our actions pursuant to these choices. From time to time we make choices that seem hurtful to others and ourselves. These events can keep us from seeing what is really in our own best interest (which is really what is best for everyone involved). We need to understand that our actions are our own responsibility, and then forgive whatever mistakes we make. These errors are mistakes, which can be corrected, and the first thing we do to correct them is admit our part in the problem. We do not have to blame someone else to make ourselves feel better. We simply own up to our behavior and let others take care of their own. We are responsible for our choices and for our forgiveness, our actions in the past and our actions today. Rather than feel that we are trapped, always doomed to repeat the same mistakes, we know that we can change the patterns of the past. Today, let us choose what we really want and then forgive the rest.

MAY 28th – DEFENSE --- I am in need of no defense. Sometimes we may feel alone and at risk. These feelings have motivated us to act in ways that perpetuate our sense of danger. We are responsible for these feelings... We should know that our feelings are the things that can immobilize us so that we cannot act. Our feelings have been responsible for many rash actions. Our defensive feelings have been the cause of much suffering. Let us determine to do something different. In the past, we may have heard someone say "You can't help how you feel" but we know right now that is not true. We are slave to defensive feelings no longer. We can change how we feel, by changing how we think. Today, examine which thoughts are leading us to any defensiveness and then ask spirit to purify these thoughts.

MAY 29th – DECISION --- I am choosing Unity. We are responsible for our thoughts. We are responsible for our choices. We can choose our thoughts...we can substitute one thought for another. We can choose Heaven or hell. We should remember that thoughts are the triggers of our feelings. We may have thought we have no control over what we think, but we do have the ability to change our thinking. While we may not be able to stop a particular thought before it comes, we certainly can decide what to do with it once we think it. Anytime a negative or unwanted thought comes to us, we can decide to change our mind. This simple idea is marvelously effective. So, today, whenever fearful thoughts occur let us just say no to those thoughts and replace them with ideas that uplift us. Right now, lets take responsibility for our decisions, making a commitment to decide for Oneness.

MAY 30th – MIND --- I am accepting Oneness. Atonement is the changing of our belief system. Our beliefs are the origins of our thoughts. Somewhere a long time ago, we got the belief that we are alone and on our own. This belief has grown and reproduced itself in a variety of other beliefs that really reflect the original belief. We have believed in the ultimate isolation of life, we have believed in lack, we have believed that we are less than some and more than others…we have believed in the unreliability of God to care for us…today, we can accept that these are erroneous beliefs. We know that they are the cause of the distressful thoughts, which trigger feelings of fear, which motivate us to act aggressively or sit paralyzed. From now on, every time one of these beliefs shows itself, let us accept Atonement (that we are all One). We can say, "My father and I are one," We can think "If God be with me, of whom shall I be afraid". We can believe: "I am one with my Source". From this belief will come healing…shared healing which can only mean Oneness.

MAY 31st – RESPONSIBLE --- I am responsible for my life. If we can see that all things, that all the situations in the world are just symbols; symbols for a reality that is hidden beyond our self-centered beliefs, we can cut through the confusion. From self-centeredness we see the symbols in a threatening light...from Spirit centeredness we will see the symbols as representative of God. We can take responsibility by seeing that every belief, thought, feeling, and action is under our direct supervision. Where we are today is a direct result of our interpretation of the symbols...every thought, word, action or inaction that we have participated in up until now is the result of our beliefs about the symbols. We no longer want to blame circumstances and events for our present reality. It is no one else's fault; we can't blame parents, teachers, friends, enemies or anyone else for where we have found ourselves. All things can be seen as symbols for good, leading to good, and resulting in good...it is totally up to us.

JUNE 1st – DECIDE - I am deciding. The choice is ours! We can choose suffering and even though it is not real, we will feel it. Every choice for suffering just delays our return to one-ness. In truth we are already in Harmony. It is only our perception and body identification that keeps us thinking that this is some future destination. This day, we can begin anew, we can decide for wholeness. We can opt for Heaven. Heaven is the ultimate safety. We can be safe by accepting the fact that we are unstained by sin and as perfect as God made us. Where we may have thought we were in conflict, let us now recognize that we have been involved in an imaginary war with ourselves. We can call off the campaign and allow ourselves to be unified. Letting go of worry and concern lets us see our fears as baseless and actually returns our attention to love. Today, at every turn let us look for Love; be sure it will be found, for it is truly already with us.

JUNE 2nd – DEFENSE – I am defenseless. We need no defense because we are not being attacked. If we can just start to remember that we are not bodies, that we are not really of this world, we will find safety. Today, we attempt a moment of quiet. The deeper we enter into the silence the clearer our memory of Home becomes. Our memory of Heaven is totally reliant on our ability to forget what is not of It. Hence…silence. We release conflict and allow our mind to mend itself. Quickly and quietly we replace viciousness with gentleness. All sense of enmity fades into the light. We need not seek ascendancy because we are already ascendant. The war that never really started is coming to an end. We give ourselves over to Goodwill, which of course is our own hidden will for ourselves. If at any time during the day we feel attacked, we can stop and remember that we are not in any real danger because the presence of God is always with us.

JUNE 3 - MINISTER – I am ministering to my brother. I am not my brother's keeper; rather, I am my brother. We remember the scripture "If you go to the altar, there to leave your gift, but are angry with your brother, go first and be reconciled with your brother and then come back and leave your gift." So many implications…and all of them point to the truth of who our brother really is. He is us and we are him…he is the Christ and therefore our spiritual identity… part of God and in part, God. Our task here in this world is to minister to our brother, thereby ministering to ourselves. When we go into the quiet and try to commune with spirit, let us ask for guidance in what we should say and what we should do. The mind filled with grievance cannot minister, the illusions must be forgiven. We can visualize ourselves going to our brother in a peaceful healing way to resolve the conflict between us, and knowing that the resolution is the message we carry. We can feel what it would be like to be in harmony. From this state of mind we go forth as ministers of God to the world.

JUNE 4 - LEAD – I am letting Spirit lead the way. When we believe we are alone we are lead astray. If we perceive conflict we are in error. Spirit can lead us to the Truth. Truth is truth; it is not a matter of perception. We may have believed that we had "our" truth and that others had theirs but this is erroneous on its face. The Holy Spirit can show us that there are no others. All true principle is but an aspect of the One principle…God is one and we are one with God. All aspects of this idea are of equal value just as all parts of God are of equal value. Anytime we believe that some condition is not true for us but that it is true for others, we have strayed. The Way leads to the understanding that all are equal parts of the integrated kingdom of Heaven. Ask for the truth, hear the truth and know that it is the truth… we live and move and have our being in God, as do all living things. That is the true message of Spirit…let that lead the way today.

JUNE 5 – HOLY – I am holy. We are perfect. With God we are perfect. Outside of God (impossible) we are sinful. Separation (impossible) is the original sin, and the generator of all other sins. The idea that everyone sins is not helpful to our enfoldment; it is an obsession with the impossible. "Sinners all" is a hopeless concept that fails to recognize our innate ability to rise above all mistakes and take whatever corrective action as necessary. If we think that missing the mark deserves a death sentence then we must change our minds accordingly. The escape from the continual cycle of life and death is accomplished by entering into the eternal now, where God is always with us. It is in the holy instant that we find revelation, which washes away all seeming sin. Let the guilty ones go, release our own shame, and be free. As we forgive our sins, forgiving our brother's as well, we come close to Heaven, we come closer to God.

JUNE 6 –PRESENCE - I am in the Presence. In the silence we enter into the Presence of perfection. We become aware that we are all a part of that Perfection. If God is perfect then must all parts of God be perfect. If God creates us then we must be perfect. But if we are prone to mistakes which cause us and others pain, how can we be part of God...or if that is possible then how can we atone for our apparent errors? Silence! Quiet these error thoughts. In spirit, which is to say in reality, we are all one and we do not make any mistakes. It is only in our body identification that errors are made. To atone for these ego errors we need only see that they do not exist in reality but only in our perception and perception can be changed. We heal the mistakes of the past by seeing that they are like wisps of fog on the morning breeze that dissipate and become invisible before the light of the sun. Now, we can enjoy the silence...basking in Christ light we are whole and healed.

JUNE 7 – GIVE – I am giving the peace that I receive. We are continually receiving and giving. Love is extended to us, so we extend it through us. Peace is given and so we give it. We accept peace of mind and then give it freely. Whatever it is that we would have we must be willing to give. Remember that the greatest gift is the vision of Christ...give this gift as it is received. See Christ within...see Christ in every brother. This is the gift that gives peace. We can stop grasping and holding...creation is trying to give us the desires of the heart. Today we can use our vision to give from the heart and see how immediately our heart is filled. We are at peace and in love, at home in the kingdom of Heaven. That which God has given can never be taken back, so relax...give and keep giving.

JUNE 8 – EXCHANGE – I am exchanging miracles. A miracle of forgiveness brings peace; today let us give this gift as we receive it. In order to be at peace we must let go of all fear. Total peace is that which we seek. It is the gift of Spirit and it is freely given. Today, let us hold nothing more important than the attainment and sharing of this gift. Let go of all other goals…there really is nothing to fear…for if we enter into this holy place we can be assured that all good things are already ours. 'Seek first the kingdom and all these will be added to you'. Release any thought of specialness. In the world we have tried to be special at the expense of others. Even the specialness we assign to others is a left-handed compliment. This is the essence of isolation. Our "specialness" has been our burden all these useless centuries. It has caused all of our fears, which have resulted in all of our so-called sins. Our sense of difference is the very state of hell, which we seek to escape. Our differences drive us to madness and war; know today that they are figments of our imagination. Here is the truth, in the kingdom there is no reason for specialness because all are wonderful and all are equal and all are therefore at peace. So we forgive the world and we receive the forgiveness that leads to peace.

JUNE 9 – HOME – I am home. We are at home, free from all fear. Freedom has always been ours, but we have opted to chain ourselves to judgment. Today we continue to practice. Our practice is simple; we see Christ in our brother and affirm that both of us are home in God. We can put our attention on the Goodness that stands before us. If at anytime you find yourself feeling threatened say to yourself: "I am home; my brother and I are one…and we are all one with God." This will set him free and in the process so also will we be free. You have heard it said: "Everyone we meet today has a gift for us and we have one for them. The freedom of spirit to give is the same freedom that in turn creates the universe. Our gifts go forth from us to expand and then return to us somehow multiplied. We will be free to the extent that we are able to grant freedom to those around us. Say it all through the day "I am free…we are free from fear…home in Heaven.

JUNE 10 – CHRIST -- I am anointed. We are the Christ. Everyone we meet today has a blessing for us. When we recognize the Christ in the one we meet, we see it in ourselves and in everyone. All of us anointed in the Spirit, We are of God, children of God, Son of God, and this is our true existence. Our dream of uniqueness has stolen our inheritance from us. Alone we do nothing, together we not only accomplish all things, but we are all things. The Christ in us forgives instantly, it recognizes that the only thing of value is Love and it extends that love through us. There is no danger here... we walk together in the light of God. Get quiet for a time; this holy presence is the very essence of stillness. Reach for it right now; take on the shining mantle that is your birthright. Cover yourself in this cloak of light and love. Allow it to enfold you...after a few moments you will come to see that you also enfold it. As within so without... you are anointed and you anoint. "Let the mind that was in Christ Jesus be in you." This is a call for permission, for God will not force anything upon us. We must allow this mind to be active in us and when we do we realize it was really ours all along.

JUNE 11 – ORIGINAL -- I am as I have been. We are as we were originally created…we have done nothing which can change the truth of our beings. We need no defense. Today we will change our mind concerning our state of affairs. In our chosen loneliness we seemingly have much to fear and much to lose. We have painted a world of threat onto the canvas of our thoughts. It is enough; let us turn from thoughts of difference and division. We can put our perception to work for the good of our very being. Seeing situations as dangerous, or seeing our brothers threatening causes one conflict after another. They are not dangerous, nor are we. Seeing threat becomes a chain of effects issuing from a nonexistent cause. Sometimes it seems like we should take up the cause against some force or some person…this cause is doomed because it is illusory. All are as they have ever been and therefore cannot have done something that warrants us taking up arms. There is only one cause and that is our purpose of forgiveness. We can forget any opinion let leads us to believe that we have altered our creation state. Any other cause that we think exists or which we think to take up is just a distraction from the truth. If there is no threat, then we do not have to defend.

JUNE 12 – EVERLASTING – I am a part of everlasting life. Life cannot die; it is only the body that we have made that dies. We are all part of an immortal whole. Sometimes it seems as if we are at odds with life and with our brothers, but this cannot be true. We are together and together we are healthy and whole. This is truly the answer to all sickness and suffering and death. All discomfort comes from our stubborn isolation. These circumstances that seem so all pervading are really just little lies we tell ourselves. Freedom and safety go together contrary to the world view of freedom sacrificed to safety. Freedom lies in the realization of our invulnerability. We are integrated into the whole life of God and when we take on that role we are instantly and eternally healed in all ways. If we were alone God would be incomplete…this cannot be true. All good things are ours in our unity.

JUNE 13 – RESTORED – I am restored. We are restored…it literally means that we are returned to our original condition. We are restored to our creator, whole and free. Consider that for a moment. We are in our original condition…mint condition so to speak. Let us allow the full implications of this to sink into consciousness. Made in the image and likeness of God you are co-creator of the universe. Our original condition is a state of perfect love. It is pure being. We are the untarnished light of God shining out to bless all living things. We walk in grace and we grace all of those with whom we walk. This is our perfect self, which is eternally one with larger Self. Again Jesus says: "Be perfect, as your father in Heaven is perfect." This is truly our restoration.

JUNE 14 – THOUGHT – I am the thought of God. We are all together in the mind of God. We do not have to "get it together". All is already in harmony. Let us let go of all thoughts that are contrary to the unity of all Life. Our bodies have been fabricated demarcations zones. They have been our un-crossable boundary that keeps us separate from life they are the playground of ego. Feeling apart from the rest of life seems natural to the body, but we need to realize that the body itself is neutral and only does as it is instructed. The ego continues to promise rewards that fall quite short of their cost. The ego is not aware of God and is afraid of the idea of God. It uses the body for self-gratification to distract the mind from its true thoughts. The ego's solution actually causes more feelings of loneliness than we had before. Spirit offers another way; it does not wish to disown the body or to harm it in any way. Spirit sees the body in its highest role, as a communications device that can return us all to the Unity. Spirit's purpose for the body is that is should communicate love. That love opens the mind so that it can be aware of the God. So, there is no sacrifice, there is just a refocusing of intention. We come together to communicate love, so that we might know it as our own true state of mind.

JUNE 15 --- GIFTS --- I am gifted. We have been blessed with life...it is our eternal gift. Today we celebrate life... giving thanks for the good that has come to us and focusing on relieving the suffering of others. Our task is to share our gifts with all. Because we are thankful for what we have, we give freely. We understand and embrace the seeming contradiction of the phrase "I keep what I have by giving it away." As we give, Creation prospers us each day in myriad ways. We celebrate the cool breeze, the gentle rain, and the refreshing fragrance of the green, growing things...all of these symbols of the gift of Life. Good continues to come to us and move through us. Let us look for ways to be a blessing to others, celebrating life by sharing it to the utmost.

JUNE 16 --- LIFE --- I am a part of all Life. Life is One and we are one with Life. This life we have is shared. There can be no separate life. All suffering arises from that erroneous sense of division. Compassion for the suffering of others must be realized in this context. Compassion may seem to be a sympathetic consciousness of others; it is feeling distress at the suffering of others together with a desire to alleviate that suffering. But true compassion is more than that; it must allow the release of suffering and a higher vision of the light in those who seem to be in pain. The Buddha said: "Fill your mind with compassion!" Knowing the interrelatedness of all life (sunyata) and the compassion (karuna) that grows out of that knowing prepare me for a life of service. This is my response to the interconnectivity of creation…to give that which I have to give. As I sit quietly and consider my oneness with the universe, I have an awakening of the spirit. I will be compassionate in all my dealing with others today. I will give service wherever I can.

JUNE 17 - GRACE - I am graced by God. Today, let us allow the grace of God to become apparent to us. As we focus on the breath in all of our interactions with the world we come to peace and an appreciation of grace. As we keep our attention on and follow the breath we are able to look deeply into life. The mind becomes a tool in the removal of suffering that is present in ourselves and in others. Calmly we see through to the truth…all suffering comes from a sense of separation, a sense of isolation. In calmness we return to that state of grace and thus alleviate our own suffering. As we look still deeper we see that all those who may have harmed us in any way whatsoever are also suffering from this fear of being alone in the dark. We see that anyone who has seemed to make us suffer is suffering themselves and we send compassion and forgiveness to them. This is grace in action. We breathe in the love of God and we breathe out the light of God. We breathe the forgiving light of God to all those who suffer, we see them surrounded in grace; we see them healed and whole.

JUNE 18 - HEART --- I am loving. Today we open our hearts to the grace of God. We open our hearts and allow the love of God to flow. The love of God, as grace, flows from the heart and returns to flow into the heart. The heart is a pump, delivering not just blood around the body but also delivering compassion to ourselves and to others. Today we reflect the grace of God by truly caring about people, even people who are fearful, angry, jealous, overpowered by addiction, arrogant, proud, miserly, selfish…the heart of grace filters out any fear of finding these unattractive things in myself and it filters out judgments of people who exhibit judgment as well. We no longer have to be afraid of pain; we can open up and allow ourselves to acknowledge our own suffering and the suffering of others. The pain can soften and purify and then be released…the experience can make us more loving and kind. We do not cling to pain, but rather experience it, bless it, and send it on its way…

JUNE 19 - UNDERSTANDING --- I am open and receptive. Today we release all need for revenge or retribution. As always our meditation is a totally non-violent, non-aggressive occupation. We empty ourselves of all need for revenge or retribution, allowing for the possibility of connecting with unconditional openness. God does not judge, nor does He punish...so neither will we. From this foundation we can change first our inner condition and then the world. This quiet wisdom is our birthright, the vast unfolding display of primordial richness, primordial openness, primordial wisdom itself. Calm and centered, we have no intention of causing harm...we are mindful of causing no harm...a sense of clear seeing descends upon us...we have respect and compassion for all that we perceive...this mindfulness is the ground of understanding and refraining from harm is the path of compassion.

JUNE 20 - SYMBOLS - I am aware of symbols. Let us see that everything that happens can be seen as a symbol for the ideal that lies beyond it. All the people of our world can be seen as representative of Christ. With the guidance of the Holy Spirit we can see the good in all. We can decide what it is that we will treasure: suffering or joy. Where your treasure is so shall your heart be also…suffering comes from the desires of the ego…bliss comes from realizing the desires of the heart. There is a great goodness in the midst of us, our talents and abilities are gifts that are calling out for expression. When we choose to give these gifts to the world they become a treasure…and we become a treasure. This is the work of the compassionate seeker, to strive to bring these inner riches to others. Let us choose to bring good to the world… through our work and our works. Let us give our treasure to life and life will give an even greater treasure to us.

JUNE 21 - SAFE - I am safe. Let us release all defense. We need not concern ourselves with protecting ourselves, because we are already under the protection of divine justice, which is to say Goodwill. As we act justly and live justly we see that justice is always present. We serve to serve, without concern for gain or reason. Meister Eckhart tells us we can work without a why, just because we are so guided…"God's ground is my ground and my ground is God's ground. Here I live on my own as God lives on his own…You should work all your works out of this innermost ground without knowing why." Our actions in service are the life-blood of compassion…"Those deeds which do not flow from within your inner self are all dead before God." In the past we may have thought that we or someone else did not deserve compassion and that justice for us would be some sort of punishment; today we know that justice is compassion, that it is the very love of God moving through us as the works of our lives and to us through the works of others.

JUNE 22 - ADMISSION -- I am not alone. In times of suffering we may struggle with many questions. We probably have found excuses for our present condition, and also found many to blame for it. It may seem as if we are at the mercy of an unmerciful world and that life seems to be conspiring against us. Alone we are powerless, in the struggles of the ego there will always be great disappointments. When we admit that self-centeredness is not the way, another path opens to us. We begin to sense the power of creation as it moves through us. As we sit quietly allowing our awareness of the presence of God to grow stronger we feel the power that is within and all around us. Today, let's make a decision to let this presence to go with us when we get up and out into the world. We allow the voice for God to guide us in all that we do. A relaxed sense of power, a focused ability to create will continually flow through us. Nothing to worry about, we are immersed in the river of life and the water is warm. Relax into it.

JUNE 23 - POWER -- I am immersed in the power of God. Let us enter into the presence of God. We are in God and God is in us. We are connected to life. Occasionally, we may think we are disconnected or "apart from" nevertheless, in truth we are linked in the never-ending web of life. We have a part to play in creation…our decision is not only whether we will play our role but also how much, how effective, how we will play it. Creation has invested itself in us…there is perfection in us. It doesn't really mean that there is a perfect place for us or a perfect job or a perfect person…it means that the perfection is in us, part of us just as we are part of it. Perfect employment means that we employ the perfection that is in us to a good end…it is of course, easier to do when the work we choose compliments your talents and abilities.

JUNE 24 - CENTER -- I am at home. We are blessed and we are a blessing; we are safe at home, free to give as required. Today we use our breath to find our way to generosity and home. We relax, release and let go. Focusing on our breath...just noticing how it works...on the in-breath we are filled; on the out-breath we just naturally relax the body. As we continue to breathe we are able to ease our minds by letting go of any worries or concerns. We simply allow these anxious thoughts to die a natural death, we simply stop holding on to them and they flow easily out from our minds. We set the spirit free by letting go of any grievances...any judgments or resentments are just weighing us down; so we simply let them go. This is an easy discipline; we can do it anywhere at anytime and with anyone. Let us reach our center right now, and let us remember that we are at home, that there is nothing to fear and therefore we can give of ourselves in whatever way is necessary.

JUNE 25 - PROCESS -- I am in process. Something is going on in us. We are involved in a great spiritual evolution that actually is restoring us to our original state. Our perceptions change as we bless our fellows and the world we see with love...we go from a perspective of isolation to one of Unity. When we realize that our fellows are blessing us each moment, we are able to give our blessing. With each decision to move in the direction of something Greater we move the process forward. With each moment of honesty we involve ourselves more fully in the ultimate Truth. No need to worry about mistakes and mis-steps...we just don't deny them, we recognize them and then we go in a better direction. We keep moving forward and upward. When things seem hard that is a reminder to keep moving forward, to remember that the path of life is ever upward. Sometimes it seems like it would be so easy to just give up...to stop trying. Let's not be confused, there is a difference between giving up the ego and giving up the ghost. When an endeavor is only about money, property or prestige, surrender is in order. When the contest is against our own best efforts it should be surrendered, when we are working toward the common welfare there is only regret in the quitting. No quitting. If the work becomes difficult, I will try to relax into it. Some struggle may seem necessary but I remember the words "Easy does it, but do it"

JUNE 26 - FREE -- I am free. We do not have to be in charge of our world. This desire for control is an effect of our fear...ultimately our fear of death. Bodies die, but we are not our bodies and so we do not die. The struggle for control of the world is just a diversion of ego from our true task of forgiving what we have seen. Divine order is in charge. Our life is in divine order. With daily surrender to the presence of God within us we become aware of order in all things. Divine order is just another term for "God's Will". Divine order means that no matter how things appear to be, there is an intention, an opportunity and a pattern of good in the midst of it. When we allow ourselves to feel the love of God, it is not hard to see the pattern. We can be at ease and able to direct our efforts to the greatest effectiveness according to the guidance we receive. Yes, it may seem that we are cogs in the machine, but know that we are intelligent cogs in the divine machine. We come to understand that we are not just seeing the patterns we are in the pattern. We are strands in the great tapestry of eternal life...we are free and safe within its weave.

JUNE 27 - ACCEPTANCE -- I am accepting. We accept responsibility for our life. Our journey is a return to Love. We can begin by accepting the thought that we are one with Love, one with Life, one with God. Once this thought is held in mind we begin to experience many gifts. We are responsible for our lives but God is always with us in our endeavors. We have nothing to complain about. On this path we need make no excuses. Excuses are just another way to complain. "I was so busy…" "I just am not feeling that well…" "I guess I just don't have 'it' today". All of these are distractions. Today, let's not make any excuses. If in the course of the day we make a mistake, let's take responsibility for it in as straightforward a manner as possible. If someone else makes a mistake, it is probably better to say nothing at all. Even if we had nothing to do with the shortcoming, it cannot help to point to others. We accept what is, and then do our best, with the help of Spirit, to facilitate a solution. No excuses.

JUNE 28 - GRACE -- I am graceful. Surrendering to the life of God within us and all around us, we are filled with grace. We surrender to the desires of the heart. Today we decide how we want life to be. We examine aspirations. We remember our ultimate Goal and review our smaller goals. We determine if they are still in alignment with our purpose of service and our mission to help alleviate suffering and the overarching goal of removing the blocks to Love. In that quiet minute, we surrender ego to that creative power within us. We allow ourselves to be embraced by the universe. We ask Spirit within to guide us in our choices. We allow the heart to shine its light on the path in front of us. There is not enough time for us to deal with having everything which catches our fancy. In choosing our goals we decide what is important and then put our focus there. Releasing the desires of the ego we embrace the desires of the heart. We know that the gift of grace allows us to move forward without fear.

JUNE 29 -- GENTLE -- I am gentle. I am gently traveling from one point of view to a higher one. I see the reality of creation. All mistakes are just errors that can be corrected. Being the recipient of God's gentle grace I can let go of any worries or concerns about getting or having. I forgive my mistakes; I forgive the perceived mistakes of others. By doing this I open myself to try new things without being afraid of failure. If at any time I start to think that I am not doing what I should be doing or I am not doing it well enough, I stop and forgive. I allow the love of God to wash over me. I relax into the Presence and allow the Power to do for me what ego can never do. I see myself moving through my day with ease and grace. All of the things that need to be done are effortlessly accomplished. Anytime I find myself in trouble, I relax again. I know that all of the power that I need is being provided. I let go and let God; I let go and let creation do its job.

JUNE 30 -- HOPE -- I am hopeful. Hope is an activator. Hope turns on faith. Hope is not wishing or fantasizing about some future event. It is not pinning our aspirations on some set of circumstances or some other person's behavior. Hope is inspiration. Hope is what happens when we notice that other people have had the same problems and challenges as us and they have overcome. My prayer will be one of trusting that all of our suffering can be undone. Today, I will also observe my brothers and sisters with trust. I will become of aware that they are extending love to me and to all of life. Their actions notwithstanding, I will extend trust and prepare to be inspired by my fellows. I will increase my trust from this inspiration and then I will extend my trust out into the world. As this process unfolds I begin to notice that we are all shining, and that we are all becoming a vision of hope for each other. Today, I will extend hope, faith and trust.

JULY 1 -- STILL -- I am still. When I am still I know that I am one with the greater whole. Unity is our home. Faith is a perceiving power. Faith is the ability for me to see clearly. Once hope has turned on my power of faith, I begin to see reality. Faith is trust, trusting in the power of God. Faith is a knowing; it is knowing that we are home in the presence of God. This knowing, this trusting puts into a state of mind in which all things are possible. It is absolute, unshakeable conviction that we are involved with the ongoing miracle of creation. This trust in and of itself makes me whole...sees only One and only Oneness. Quieting the mind is freedom from fear and the release of dread. This state of mind is the opening of the kingdom of heaven, which is our home.

JULY 2 -- INTER-DEPENDENT -- I am inter-dependent. We have grown from dependence through independence to interdependence. Creation connects and relies on that connection for further extension. As we call love onto our awareness we come together. Let us hold on to hope, faith, healing and not waste time or energy on worry. Spirit can instruct body and mind. In the centered calm of our meditation, we feel body and mind in synchronicity, all things working together for good. Right now, just as we are, we are magnificent creations of an ever-present, all-providing God. Spirit directs our mind, which sends thoughts of restoration to the body and spirit, directs the body, which, in turn, sends feelings of well being back to our mind.

JULY 3 -- ABUNDANCE -- I am abundant. We inherit all there is…all Light, Love and Spirit are ours. We share life. We are in the flow of life. No matter what is going on around us, the Holy Spirit is continually lifting us up and reminding us that we have Everything. We are free to pursue goals and aspirations, which are also the challenges of the moment that can cause anxiety and upset, but as we return our thoughts to God we are calmed. The Holy Spirit is the bridge that connects us with our inheritance and brings the peace that passes all understanding. Let us release any outer distractions, letting go of worry and fear. Open and receptive to the all of the good in creation, we are prosperous and abundant…the reality of heaven reflects into our lives in the world. At peace, all of our decisions are wise and well considered. I do not have to rush into anything; we relax and let God guide us in whatever is ours to do this day.

JULY 4 -- RESTORATION -- I am being returned to my former State. Peace is my natural state. God is One and I am one with God. Reality is oneness, and oneness brings love and peace. There is one God and that God is one. God is everywhere present; there is not one place where God is not. God is in everything and everything is in God. This is such a peaceful, comforting thought. God is One and I am one with God. In regards to the desires of my heart, I understand that these true desires come from God. Through the use of my talents and abilities they come to pass in a natural way. Consider these symbols: The birds of the air are cared for because they do not try to be other than birds. The flowers of the field are clothed because they play their present role as flowers. In the same way, all the good that is ours comes to us through Being. Good comes to us through being who and what we are. God is One and I am one with God…at peace in God.

JULY 5 -- SANITY -- I am sane. The safety of the world depends on our sanity. Sanity is soundness of mind, wholeness and health. My mind is healed and through this the world is healed. There is a healing power within us. Hold an image in mind in which we are all immersed in the healing light of God. We are blessed by health and wholeness. The body is the temporary vessel of the Holy Spirit. The body can reflect the wholeness of spirit or it can reflect division and conflict. Sanity and salvation are the same. Wholeness and health...health of mind is the realization of wholeness. Our mission is to extend sanity from within out into the world...thus saving it!

JULY 6 --- WILLING --- I am willing to bless and be blessed. Today let us be willing to do our part in creation, let us be willing to bless the world. Ambitions and goals, hopes and aspirations can be means to bless or to further separate. Understand that these good desires come from divine mind. Temporarily we each have unique collection of talents and abilities and these attributes bless ourselves and then bless the world in turn. We just need to keep the priorities in order. If we are willing to do the work then the desires of my heart come into manifestation as blessings. That work is really just being, being whom we are in every situation that occurs. If we set aside fear and apprehension we will be blessed and we will bless. Let us be willing to do so.

JULY 7 - LIGHT - I am shining. We know that we cannot successfully serve two masters. We must be single minded to achieve our goals. Single-mindedness means focused on God and the peace that comes from God. Single- mindedness means not focusing on money or material things, but rather on the principle of abundance behind them. Release any desire to have and to own. Seek rather to participate in creation. The indwelling spirit knows what we need is providing it, we only need focus on receiving it. The creative power within us can produce money and material things, but we find them unfulfilling and life becomes a continual cycle of wanting and getting and wanting again. Instead of looking for what we can get, let us consider giving that Light that is within us, and more of all good things will automatically come our way.

JULY 8 - LOVE - I am filled with the love of God. Today let us engage in the reality of living beyond the limitations of the ego. Let's take the time to get in touch with our hearts. Just take a moment right now to notice that there is already a strong connection between heart and brain. We can feel the love of Spirit moving through us. This conduit of spirit allows us to use both of these great faculties in concert with each other. Let us allow our feeling nature to be wed to our thinking nature. The truth of life is found when the disparate parts of us come together in harmony. As we allow the love of God to work through us, and then divine will becomes our own true will for ourselves. As we stay aware of that loving presence we are able to extend it.

JULY 9 - JOY - I am happy. We can choose happiness. Today, we stay the course...we decide for bliss. With each loving choice we move in the direction of our desire. Whatever our daily activities may be, we stay aware of our happy mission and joyful purpose. We are here to be helpful. When we are helpful we are joyful. We keep service in the front of our mind at all times. We know that in order to move in the direction of the divine we must change beliefs, thoughts, feelings and actions. Let us release any rituals and habits that may have established that do not contribute to our purpose. We pursue positive change by focusing on the greater mission. We understand that only through service to others will we be able to overcome the obstacles to peace that ego places in our path. Let us keep on the path, giving and receiving happiness and joy.

JULY 10 - CHILD - I am a child of God. We are all God's children. In order to fully realize our true identity we must be willing to see the value of each one. Let us make a commitment, this day, to be aware of the value of the others in our life. We are connected to all of those who are not so close and all of those whom are close to us. We are all part of the web of life and each part has tremendous value. We share our humanity and our divinity with people of all races, cultures, and ethnic backgrounds. Keeping this in mind teaches the value of each of us, and the gifts we bring to the world. We can also cultivate our sense of connection to all life, not just the people but also all living things. In this way we stay aware of our responsibility to life as a whole.

JULY 11 --- DESTINY --- I am willing to meet my destiny. Do you believe in destiny? We are not talking about pre-destination. We are speaking of destiny as potential. Our ultimate destiny is to return to God, and everything thing we do on this spiritual journey moves our perception towards that end. Today, let's develop and maintain a sense of destiny. As we grow in awareness we become examples and leaders to those around us. Great leaders inspire others to the extent that they are willing to reach out in the present to a vision of the future and can embrace that view. When we begin to stand firmly in this moment and reach out into the future with vision we become magnets, which pull us all forward. We become agents of change for good and we draw people of like mind to us.

JULY 12 — LESSON --- I am willing to teach and to learn. To truly use this tremendous power of will for the good of all we must become involved in teaching what we need to learn. We start by focusing on becoming the change we want to see. We believe and we commit to our belief. We can then, if we are so guided, become active in rebuilding the political landscape. We may start to work with a new economic model, one based on what's best for everyone involved. To weave a new social fabric with the common welfare in mind, to reinvent the nature of education, these are the building blocks of the life we seek. We seek this not just for ourselves but also for the good of all. We immerse ourselves in the river of life, we flow in the direction of our talents and abilities, and we do not fight the currents of our temporary uniqueness. In this river the gifts of the individuals come together to join with the greater gifts of oneness and every living thing benefits. Teach will to learn will; practice willing your life and you live the life you will.

JULY 13 --- FUTURE --- I am turning it over. Today, let us give the future into the care of that Power greater than our small selves. Let us seek the wisdom of the ages. The spiritual literature of all the various faiths throughout time has been showing us the way back to God. They all advise staying present, forgiving the past and releasing worry over future events. Finding this great wisdom will not come from literal readings of these ancient texts. We know that the literal story is just the tip of the iceberg; we must dive deep into the words and allow our intellect to interpret and then allow spirit to inspire our heart. We are all part of One Mind. We share the mind of Creation; we really already have all the wisdom of the ages at our beck and call. Our seeking is really just remembering…it is just putting together the fragments into a coherent whole. So, as we look for wisdom, we should be listening to the words of those we meet and we should be paying attention to the way these words affect our hearts. Seek the wisdom that is available right now…through the written word, the spoken word and the silent word of the heart.

JULY 14 --- GRATEFUL - I am grateful. We are the love of God in action. We express our gratitude by extending love as a continual practice. In the past we may have seen ourselves as "less than". We might have felt shame or guilt over some behavior or shortcoming. We have learned that guilt is only good as a signal not to repeat the behavior. We are aware that changing behavior on a permanent basis means changing beliefs, thoughts, feelings and actions. Focus on being the image and likeness of God and begin to give love to life. The love of God extends Itself into the world as me. In total gratitude we accept the fact that we are all part of God and God is part of us. Our perception of the past has been in error...we correct that error by gratefully seeing who we really are...Love in action.

JULY 15 --- JUDGEMENT --- I am judging rightly. As we see others, we see ourselves. Today, let us see everyone in the light of God. From time to time we may see others in a negative light, a dark light, or perhaps a shadow. We have judged them harshly and listed their character flaws... to ourselves and to whoever else might listen. This is not wisdom or right judgment. It condemns us all. All the people we see, all of the people in the world are all of equal value. All are brothers. Today, make a commitment to see them as they are...surrounded in the light and love of God. I see that all of us are iterations of the divine. As Meister Eckhart reminds us "all creatures are words of God, and God is still speaking". God is in us and we are in God.

JULY 16 --- MIND --- I am discerning. We allow our mind to work in our heart and we are blessed. We can release the need for the approval of others, knowing that our reward is in healing ourselves and thereby healing the world. We have a wonderful capacity for deep thought. Today, let us not drown in it. Intellect needs to be tempered by feelings. As helpful as analysis can be, to be truly wise we must allow mind to connect with heart. This is all symbolism of course and the important thing to realize is that all of our efforts are focused on returning to the pure Love of God. Changing our thought process will put us in a position where we can be gathered back into the arms of Spirit. So we want to stop seeing things in black and white. We allow intuition to inform our knowledge. We take care not to let either emotions or intelligence to have sole reign in our life and affairs. We can work out a partnership between them...a marriage, so to speak. Cosmic Mind is our mind, it is integrated and whole, so we listen to what it has to say with humility. As Emerson said "There is one mind common to all individual persons...and by "lowly" listening we shall hear the right word". Surely that word will be love.

JULY 17 – PARDON - I am pardoned. "All things are lessons God would have us learn." This quote encourages us to continue our education. As we move through this life-long learning, we keep an ear open to inner knowledge. In our lives there will be many mistakes that we can learn from...the benefit of the lesson is not acquired through guilt or shame. All of the facts and the figures are of little value without proper discernment. We are already filled with infinite knowing; all of our pursuit of learning is just a remembering process or perhaps a sorting out process. Our meditation is the process by which we continue to get in touch with the indwelling spirit, who has all wisdom. We begin by knowing that God is all good; and that love will meet every need, that kindness is what is most called for. We read, we pray, we listen, and we meditate. We learn to extend ourselves in new ways. We discern God where we did not before. Book by book, prayer by prayer, we educate ourselves to trust, to love, to be, to do.

JULY 18 --- TRANSCENDENCE --- I am transcending. Today, I release all of the old concepts of God and of us. God is not a body and we are not bodies. God as some "super person" with x-ray vision and the power to grant wishes. We are not in need of granted wishes. As Son of God we are already blessed with all things. God is present in all and all is present in God. This may be a very different vision than we were brought up with. Divine wisdom gives us the ability to transcend these restricting, fearful thoughts. Good judgment has us seeing that God is present always and in all ways. God is all knowing, but what is more, God in us is all knowing. God is wisdom itself and we are, therefore wise. Creation is totally present everywhere and every-when. It is fully present and totally involved in the smallest particle and the largest galaxy. We embrace these new ideas as we transcend the old ones.

JULY 19 --- HAPPY --- I am happy. Happy are we, who have found wisdom. The Proverb (3:13-19) tells us that those who find wisdom are happy. Elation, even glee can be said to be a side effect. This is a far cry from the picture of somber old folks filled with some kind of sour wisdom. Further, we are told that the income from wisdom is better than silver or gold. That she (wisdom seems to a female trait here) is more precious than jewels. No desire can compare with her. The benefits from wisdom are long life sprinkled with riches and honor. Her ways are ways of pleasantness and all her paths are peace. Wisdom is likened to a tree of life for those who lay hold of her; those who hold her fast are called happy. Then stunningly the proverb finishes by saying "The Lord by wisdom found the earth (mother); by understanding he established the heavens (father)". So happy are we who have formed a partnership within us between love, faith and understanding.

JULY 20 --- OPEN --- I am open and trusting. Today we open mind and heart. Before us is the infinite field of possibility. There are so many options available that it can seem overwhelming. We really do get to decide what our lives in this world will be. The most important thing is to be open to guidance from Spirit. "All things work together for good to those who love God" This quote tells us that if we extend love to God and God's creations all events and circumstances will coalesce into goodness. So, we surrender ego, allow hope to activate faith, align our will with goodwill, and decide for right judgment. We open our minds to the wonderful possibilities and we open our hearts to the opportunities to give love and service that these possibilities represent. We open our mind and heart to good.

JULY 21 --- BEFORE --- I am humble before God. God stands before us. Before we were, God is. Awareness of our place in the scheme of things is essential for our ongoing well being. We are part of God, but we are not the whole of God. God is the whole of us, but we are a part of God. Eternal life, love and light are all ours. This is all well and good, and as it should be. We have a place in Universal Mind and we always will have. God is our source, and his pattern is our pattern. God is Creator we are creative. Being humble means both knowing and taking our place. Our job is the same as God's job, only on a smaller scale. Our job is to shine the light of creation on everyone we meet and into everything that we do. Our place is wonderful and honorable and excellent to consider.

JULY 22 --- MYSTERY --- I am in awe. I marvel at the mysteries of life. Much is unknown to us. What happens exactly when this body dies? Where do we go? What happens next? Do we come back? Did we ever really leave? These answers to these questions are unknowable from our present perspective. We all have opinions and ideas concerning these things, but we can't know for sure. There are many other wonders that we cannot yet understand. The universe is awesome but this does not mean it has to be scary. These mysteries need not frighten us when we remember that no matter what the various answers are, the main answer is that God stands under all. Ultimately we will return from this relative world to the absolute world of Spirit. When and how this will happen are hidden to us as long as we remain in the relative world but we can take comfort in the fact that Creation is in the midst of all, known and unknown.

JULY 23 --- INSPIRED --- I am inspired. God is love and we are all love. Observing with open ears, eyes, mind and heart we can be inspired by the words and deeds of others. We remember that we all share the nature of God. Someone once said "show me don't tell me". This, of course, conveys the sense that we would rather follow someone's good example than take their advice. Actually, both can be helpful...even the person who is not "walking the walk" may inspire us with uplifting words. We can just treat the words like affirmations that have not yet come into manifestation. We can visualize the person acting in the same manner in which they speak. Today, let's give people the benefit of their own positive words treating them like good intentions. At the same time let us release them from their negative words and actions through forgiveness. See them, as they really are son/daughter of God just like us.

JULY 24 --- INSPIRING --- I am inspiring? I share my ideas freely. As we allow ourselves to be vulnerable, we become more trusting overall. As we share our feelings and our ideas openly, our intimacy allows a stronger connection to our loved ones. It is a good practice to be free in sharing our feelings but we should also freely give our ideas. At home, at school, in the workplace we have a part to play in the ongoing development of the larger organism. Great new things begin with single ideas. To think that our ideas are not good enough or that they will not be well received keeps us from exercising our creative powers. It really is up to us to give what is ours to give in every situation. We want to be discreet and not overbearing but let's not hold back! Most of the time, we know more than we give ourselves credit for. We have an intuition that should not be denied. Let's give others the benefit of our insights and freely share our ideas.

JULY 25 --- EVOLVE --- I am consciously evolving. We are works in progress. The bumper sticker "Be patient with me, God is not finished with me yet" is a partial reflection of truth. Creation is at work in us at the sub-conscious level and through us at the conscious level. Indeed, God is not done with us. We are continuing to unfold and become that which we were designed to be. We must recognize however that much of this unfolding can be done through conscious thought and action on our part. When we see that we live and move and have our being in God and that the relative world in which we now find ourselves is full of possibility we are able to start making choices and taking actions that move us toward that which we truly desire. What an exciting idea, total freedom to be and to become that which we are meant to be. Every time we consciously extend love, through creativity or through kindness we evolve and grow.

JULY 26 --- UNDERSTAND --- I understand. I understand that I am related to all of creation. We are in right relation with the Universe. God is continuing to create, and we are co-creators with him. God is the infinitely large and infinitesimally small. God is outward bound and inward seeking. Our lives…our beliefs, thoughts, feelings and actions may seem very small indeed compared to the vastness of the universe, but they are no less wonderful and no less a part of the beauty of creation. Right relation with the universe is a sense of belonging. Trust abounds when we know that we are an integral part of this ongoing enterprise. We sense that our place is always assured. We can take chances; step out on faith knowing that while we may lose the day, we cannot lose our place. We belong to and we are treasured by our Father. We come to the understanding that we are intimately related with everyone and everything in the great and grand universe.

JULY 27 - HABIT - I am changing. In the relative world we are changing; its best if we embrace the change. Our perspective needs to be altered so that we can come to a view that sees past the relative to the Absolute. We want to change until we reach the Unchangeable. We are more than our worldly habits. In the past we may have been afraid that we would never be able to escape our bad habits. We may have identified ourselves with our quirks and foibles, or perhaps viewed ourselves like characters in a bad movie. Today, we know that we can change. We can order our behavior and our lives as we wish. Let us release all fear of change, embracing new ideas and positive habits. From time to time we are getting signs and signals that something wonderful is underway in us. We know that there are still nagging little habits, but we can see there is a solution. As we continue to embrace change and practice new ways, our habits begin to change. The outer is all about change, the inner, the deep is changeless.

JULY 28 - GOOD - I am good. I realize the goodness in me. It is important to know that the real me does not change… it does not need to change. Only the surface behaviors… fear based reactions and such need to change. As I move through the process to change these things, I hold to the fact that at my core, I am good. By holding to the positive, I am strengthened to change the negative. In my meditation, I visualize myself in this magnificent oneness with Creation. I see myself getting proper rest, eating the right foods in the right quantity, and staying physically active and mentally alert. I move through my day giving proper service in every situation that occurs. Today, I embrace the good…when the negative begins to come forth I bless it on it's way and allow it to go.

JULY 29 - IMAGE - I am who I am. Today, we decide who and what we want to be. There is an image of who we really are in our hearts. It is the picture of the kind of people we want to be. We know that what we really want is to be more loving, happier people. We want to be thankful and filled with the spirit of God, We want to be a decisive people who move into right action without fear, and we see ourselves forgiving the past so that we can know the present. Today, let's put these attributes on order with the divine…Let's order what we want to see in our lives. Let us decide what we want. Let's hold that image in our minds of the child of God that we were meant to be.

JULY 30 - ORDERLY - I am in order. Although sometimes it doesn't seem so, order is the way of the universe. No matter how chaotic things may appear, God's will, expressing, as divine order is available to us. The opportunity for good always exists in the present moment. Every person, every situation, every thing that happens, it's all in divine order. Life will flow from good to greater good as we become more receptive to the possibilities of creation that are always present. We have free will, which is the ability to choose between, Goodwill and something less than that. It really is up to us; no one else can decide for us and no one else can cheat us out of experiences (good or bad). They are ours, and ultimately, we are in charge of our lives. Order is present right now. Once we fully appreciate that process, we come to the understanding that we can't be separated from it and that our lives are cradled in divine order.

JULY 31 - RECOGNIZE - I am recognizing the truth. I lay aside my grievances. Let's see that we are holding our brothers hostage to our complaints. Just take a moment right now to picture a person in your life that you are in conflict with. The grievances come quickly to mind. Now, just allow you to lay those complaints aside and then see this person in a new light. Notice how they have changed. Recognize them as Son of God, just like you. Allow yourself to feel the love you have had all along for this person. Know, that if you decide to leave your complaints where you lay them, you can continue to feel this way. Sometimes, it is tempting to blame others for problems. These grievances block us from the good that God has for us…they actually keep us locked into victim mentality. Let's stop playing the victim; let us lay aside our grievances.

AUGUST 1 - RECREATION - I am relaxing. Let go of all dysfunction of mind. We need not be interested in thoughts of worry, escape or fantasy. We all need recreation, but true recreation is playing, resting and building up of strength. Fantasy is not recreation, but rather, a waste of creative energy because its main tenet is that it can never really happen. All of the energy spent in escape from reality can be channeled into true creation. Putting the resources of Mind together to creating that which we desire. Obsession with anything is a waste and should be eliminated like any other waste…flushed from the mind. We can allow any thoughts of escape; any obsessed thinking flow out and away from us. We do not have anything to escape from; the common abundance of the universe is our abundance. All of the Good of God is ours to share. Relax and let go of all dysfunction of mind.

AUGUST 2 - INSPIRED - I am inspired by the Holy Spirit. Spirit laid the foundation of who I am. Positive change comes naturally from creative thought and action. Today, I open my mind to all of the possibilities. I am open and receptive to the inspiration of the Holy Spirit that inhabits me. I will allow this spirit to guide me in what I should say and what I should do. There will be challenges throughout the day, but I know that they are just good things in disguise. I know how to eliminate the negative and see the good. From the foundation of spirit comes opportunity to be creative in handling all of the possibilities that will arise this day. I see all the new people and situations that come to me today are blessings and I will treat them as such.

AUGUST 3 - READINESS --- I am ready for whatever is next. Knowing I am cared for and protected within the love of God, I am ready for whatever is next. I am ready to allow this presence to do for me what my ego could not do. I am ready to be healed at a deep level. I am ready to allow this presence to lift me up and move me into the realm that until now was just unrealized potential. I am willing to be made whole and well. I am fully prepared to begin a new life unfettered from the limitations of the past. I am not sure exactly what is next, but I know that it will be good. I know that what is next will be for my greater good and the good of everyone else. I am ready for whatever is next.

AUGUST 4 - ELIMINATE --- I am in the flow of life. Today, I eliminate false images of myself. I have been worshipping false idols. I have been putting my attention on the material world, on getting things to make me feel better. That's because previously, I may have been confused about my identity but now I am seeing more clearly. I am a part of.... a part of the family, the neighborhood, the community, the world, the universe. Where as I may have thought I was apart from all these things, I am beginning to realize, I am intimately connected to all of them. I am an irreplaceable part of God. Today, every time the old images come to mind, I eliminate them, I allow them to flow away and I replace them with a picture of myself being at one with Creation.

AUGUST 5 - RENOUNCE --- I am free. I renounce my grievances. Sometimes life can be full of complaints...it is easy to find something wrong, it is easy to judge others and to judge situations as negative. It is tempting to blame others or perhaps to blame circumstances for seeming problems. These grievances block me from the good that God has for me...they actually keep me locked into victim mentality. I am tired of playing the victim, so today I renounce my grievances, I don't want them anymore. Every time I think of being put upon, I tell myself the truth. I am free from resentment and regret.

AUGUST 6 - RELEASE --- I am healed. I release all disease from my body. True prosperity includes total health of the body. If I am in need of healing I take the time to visualize any sickness leaving my body. I do not hate the microbe or the virus; I just ask them to move out of my body. I do not try to harm them in any way. I do not fear the disease but rather extend love to it, and then send it on its way. I deal with any physical pain I may be feeling in a similar way. I relax and allow the disorder to flow quickly and completely out and away from my body. I allow the healing love of God to restore my body to health and wholeness.

AUGUST 7 - LET GO --- I am letting go. Let us release all concern for what will happen in the future. Peace and plenty are our natural states. Any time we allow fear to project we suffer. Giving tomorrow into the hands of spirit we are free to be here now. There is no need to escape, there is really nothing to escape, we can just relax into the present moment. Right now everything is as it should be. We know that problems will come, but if we stay aware we are able to accept and deal with whatever comes. Suffering will occur, again we practice present awareness with acceptance and then just let it go. Grasping will never maintain the happiness it promises; so we release our grip and live moment to moment. Avoidance will fail, but acceptance of present reality will succeed. Let it go, let it all go, the pleasant and the unpleasant; don't worry something else is about to happen!

AUGUST 8 - WELCOME ---I am receptive. I welcome the spirit of plenty. I welcome new thoughts and new life. I welcome the prosperity that comes naturally from creative thought and action. Today, I open my mind to all of the possibilities. I am open and receptive to the inspiration of the Holy Spirit that inhabits me. I will allow this spirit to guide me in what I should say and what I should do. I welcome all the experiences this day has to offer. Some will come disguised as trouble, but today I know how to eliminate the negative and see the good. I welcome the opportunity to be creative in handling all of the possibilities that will arise this day. I welcome all new people and situations that come to me today, knowing that they all represent the abundance of Creation.

AUGUST 9 - CONSERVATIVE --- I am a true conservative. Today, let's focus on what it means to be a true conservative. A true conservative is conscious of the fact that he or she is steward of the earth. We all have some responsibility to the planet. We are paying attention to what we acquire, consume and then discard. Prosperity does not mean having enough to waste. Let us realize that conserving resources and energy is part of prosperous thinking. We conserve energy and resources. We are good stewards. We have been entrusted with this stewardship so let us prove trustworthy. We are up to the task, and always looking for new ways to accomplish it. Our mantra for the day is "I am a true conservative."

AUGUST 10 --- CONFIDENCE --- I am confident in the strength of God in me. The strength of God is with us and manifests through us. This strength in us is an untapped well of good fortune. We live and move and have our being in a Creation that has invested us with an overflowing abundance of strength. This strength is the ability to do what is called for in our lives. Quiet confidence is our Strength. Be confident in the presence of God in us. Know that Spirit is continually renewing our ability to deal with whatever may occur. We can relax and let go of any worry. The power of creation is at work in us. As we give ourselves to it, this power is calls more and more of our good into manifestation. "We are strong in God". This thought instills confidence as we move forward in our day.

AUGUST 11 --- ANTICIPATION --- I am anticipating good things. Today, expect the best. At every moment there is a choice to be made. We can choose for the common welfare or we can choose self-centeredness. No matter how challenging the events of the day, the good outcome is really dependent on the choice we make. If our decisions come from love and inclusion, all things will work together for good. Choices made from a lack perspective will ultimately result in lack. Centered in love we can realistically anticipate good results. We can overcome obstacles in an easy and relaxed manner. We meet the challenges of the day squarely because we don't have any ulterior motives. Goodwill in our mind leads to goodwill being done in the world which in turn shows us good results.

AUGUST 12 --- INTERACT --- I am interacting. Reaction usually leads to more problems. There is a little space in which we can take refuge before we act. It is a space of awareness. A stop, a pause, a moment in which to examine what is really happening. Our proper course is always laid out like a path. Our path is the way of service, which cannot be found in an angry retort or an aggressive act. Our past reactions are our responsibility as are our present actions. We have the ability to not respond to upset with more upset, but rather to pause and then interact in an appropriate way. Today let us consider the consequences of decisions before we move into action, always trying to be aware of our interconnection.

AUGUST 13 --- FORGIVENESS --- I am forgiving. Through the love of God, in me, I forgive. There is a great Love in me. It is that spark of light in my heart, through which all things are possible. It is this light that goes forth from me to bless the world I see. All of my prosperity, all of my abundance comes to me as a direct result of my sending forth this love. I give the love that I am, and the giving rewards me over and over again. The one thing that blocks me from giving and receiving is being locked into the past. It is regret and resentment that steal my good from me. So today, through the love of God in me, I forgive the past…

AUGUST 14 - CHANGE --- I am determined to see things differently. I am going to change the way I see. I am tired of being locked into the past and I am tired of reacting to life based on the patterns of the past. Today, I am going to change my mind...I am going to see things differently. If I am anxious or afraid, I release those feelings into God's care. I take comfort in the Presence and Power of my Creator. I no longer hold anyone else responsible for my situation. If I really want to change my life I must see it differently. So, today I decide to change my mind and my vision. I see only love, only good, only opportunity for more good. This may seem difficult or even unrealistic at times but I am determined to see the good of God wherever I look because I know that is the truth.

AUGUST 15 -- GUILTLESS --- I am guiltless. We are at peace to the extent that we forgive mistakes. We are guiltless, the mistakes that we have made are just that, mistakes, and they can be corrected. The errors of yesterday can be healed with a generous application of love today. In the past we may have held onto feelings of guilt and remorse because we thought that we needed to be held to account for our many shortcomings. Today, we can understand that being accountable means that we first take responsibility for our actions, then do what is necessary to repair the harm and finally we release ourselves from the bondage of guilt. Holding to guilt is a sure way to hold onto old patterns. It sets us up for repeating the same mistakes over and over again. So, today, we forgive our mistakes and move on, opening the way for new experiences.

AUGUST 16 --- INNOCENT --- I am innocent. I forgive all those who may have harmed me in anyway whatsoever. I release anyone who ever thought, did or said any negative thing to me…I release them from judgment. I let them go right now. As I see myself as guiltless, so must I see my brothers and sisters innocent. As I forget the transgressions of others I begin to remember Heaven. I can now see us all in the light of God's love. At times I may have found some false comfort in blaming and condemning others, but I must understand that this negative judgment only locks all of us into a continuing cycle of alienation and separation. Right now, I see only the good; I let go of all wrongs. I am free of the need to judge others, and so I forgive them and begin to see them differently. Today, I forgive and forget…so that I can remember God.

AUGUST 17 -- HEALING --- I am healing. I invite the presence of God to make itself known in my mind and I begin to heal. Knowing when it is appropriate to ask for forgiveness and how to ask is essential to this process. Whenever I have done anything for which I am sorry, I rely on God to give me the power to immediately take responsibility for my action. If so guided, I ask the person I harmed to forgive me...sometimes I ask them directly, sometimes I ask only in prayer. This means that I ask them to hold me in the same light and esteem that they did before the event occurred. The healing partially occurs because I am humble and able to admit the mistake. The healing partially occurs because I do not blame the person I harmed for the harm I caused. This may seem like common sense, but I know that in the past, I have blamed others for the things that I have done…. no longer…I am healed from my errors in the here and now because I am able to see them for what they are.

AUGUST 18 - FREEDOM --- I am free of the past. I have put the past to rest. I have given the past and the future into God's care. I have forgiven myself, I have forgiven my brothers, and I have forgiven events and circumstances. Relying on the power of God, I am free to be and to do whatever is called for in this day. Whenever I participate in an act of forgiveness, I make all things new again. It is a new day and I am a new person. All the things, which held me into the patterns of the past, have been washed away. I set all others and myself free from the slavery of the blame game. All worries and concerns are revealed in their true nature. I find, as did Jacob, that everything that I wrestle with is just God in disguise and that if I release it I get a blessing.

AUGUST 19 --- FLOW --- I am in the flow of life. Remembering that we are the children of God, we are free to access all of the Good in the universe. The abundance of creation flows through us. All of the blocks to prosperity have been removed. All of the impediments to abundance have been cleared away. We can now live in the all-encompassing flow of God's good. Love flows unchecked through our spirit. Creativity flows unimpeded through our mind. Health flows freely through the body. Through active involvement with love: creativity, good health, and prosperity blossom. We allow the love of God to inspire us and to fill us with the energy to create. We extend blessings and in return we receive all of the blessings that Creation has for us. We keep ourselves centered in the flow of life, no longer living on the edges. We are in the middle of river, living and loving, participating and observing, giving and receiving, flowing with the abundance of eternal life.

AUGUST 20 - ALIVE --- I am alive with the life of God. The life I am experiencing is part of universal life. I feel it moving in and through me. If I am experiencing fear or lack or upset of any kind it is because I have put my attention on illusion. The Life of Love is happening right now. This life is the very energy of creation. I turn my thoughts to that ever-present life of God. That life is the source of all happiness and joy. I am truly prosperous and true prosperity is the absolute supply of everything that I have need. If I need healing, I trust that the life of God in me is filling my body with healing light. If I need help with a financial situation, I let this life fill my mind with divine ideas, which will guide me to an overcoming. The energy of me is my life and the way I extend that energy determines my life experiences. Whatever my want or need, I understand that life is not a constant state of striving but rather it is the medium in which I receive and give and receive yet again.

AUGUST 21 - DAILY --- I am in this day. I stay in this day. I make a decision to allow this day to unfold and become whatever it will. Sometimes I lose my way and I begin wishing for some future reality in which I have no concerns about money or material things. I need to remember that my ongoing movement through life is the path upon which all prosperity unfolds. I am prosperous when I practice the presence of God. I am prosperous because the Holy Spirit energizes me, because I am guided by divine wisdom, because I am loving and loved. It is all here for me today. I do not have to wait for some pending event or circumstance. I am rich today…everything I have need of has already been given…this day is sufficient unto itself.

AUGUST 22 - MOMENT --- I am in the moment. I live in this moment, which in reality is the only time there is. In this moment miracles are happening, they are happening to me and those around me. This is the Holy Instant. Flowers are blossoming; life and love are being extended ever outward. New life is occurring around me and life is continuing in me. If I keep myself in this moment I will notice many wonders. I am ready for a miracle. I keep my mind and heart open to the divine presence. And I see it being expressed; I feel it extending to me, through me, and as me. In this moment I am infinitely blessed, in this moment I am intimately connected to creation, and in this moment I am rich.

AUGUST 23 - FOCUS --- I am focused. I focus on what is important, right now. I put my focus on what is in front of me right now. Any person who stands before me has a gift for me and I have a gift for them. Any situation that is unfolding is just another opportunity to experience Goodwill. Focused on right now it is easy to hear Spirit's voice. As time stretches forward, I keep my mind stayed on what is at hand. I give my attention to my place in the universe. I do not live apart from the rest of life. I am part of a system, an environment which can reflect the kingdom of heaven. I am part of a living system, which really is God. I lovingly and thoughtfully contribute to creation by remaining harmonious with all the life around me. I center myself in my role…I give what is mine to give…I know that my giving will be appreciated and reciprocated by all of life. Today, I focus on what is important.

AUGUST 24 - MINDFUL --- I am mindful. As the day unfolds, I stay mindful. I pay attention to my actions. I feel my feelings. I notice my thoughts. I am aware of my beliefs. I appreciate the beauty that is all around me. As I walk upon the earth, I sense the ground under my feet. I revel in my movement through the air. My body is a finely tuned machine and I love its action in all that it does. I am grateful for my body's ability and agility. I feel a reserve of strength that is always available when it is needed. My mind is a wonderful instrument and I marvel at its precision. My mind is adaptable and responsive, it can adapt instantly to changing circumstances. Most important I am in touch with Spirit. I stay open and receptive to the divine guidance. Spirit is always leading me to my unfolding Good, so I stay mindful.

AUGUST 25 - CORRECTION --- I am correcting errors. I make corrections where necessary. I am not afraid to admit my wrongs. When I make mistakes, I stop and correct the error. I am no longer bound by the past. I forgive and clean the slate. I let go of the past and begin anew. Every time that I make a correction, I open a new opportunity for growth and for the further unfolding of my spirit. I choose to exercise my spiritual power and potential. This power enables me to become a better, wiser, healthier and more prosperous person than I was before. I experience growth through the use of correction. I choose not to hide my mistakes any longer. I carry with me the understanding I have gained from the experience, but I let go of all guilt and regret. I release myself and all others from the limitations of error. I begin anew, right now.

AUGUST 26 -- IMAGINATION -- I am imaginative. Today we release all of our vain imaginings; we let go of our fearful judgments and embrace peace. We can see an image of peace. When we think of peace, what does it look like? We can actually imagine perfect peace. Whatever our image is, we can make it so! Form mental pictures of a perfect world, a loving and abundant place, and God's perfect world. We can clearly see all people and ourselves around the world living in peace and prosperity. We can see us all living in harmony with all life. See the planet healed. We have the ability to envision a garden where we may have seen destruction. We become aware that we are caretakers of the world. We are careful with the Earth, remembering that it is a symbol for that which lies beyond it. We are privileged to conserve energy and resources. We can image all of these things, knowing they can become reality...hold to these visions with faith.

AUGUST 27 -- VISION – I am seer. We have the gift of divine vision. Let us use divine vision to see that we are safe and sound. There is nothing to fear. We are able to use our thoughts to create a new reality. Have a vision of unity for everyone. See an abundance of good for the entire world. Know that we can help this vision become reality. Sit quietly, feel the heart fill with love. When it is filled to overflow, extend this stream of love out into the world. See family and friends receiving this love as a continuous stream of light. We are just facilitating, we can trust God to give them their own vision and show them how to express their own gifts. Expand this vision to see the light moving over the community, blessing and awakening all of those whom it touches. The vision grows still larger as the light extends across the country, healing divisions as it does. The light encircles the planet bringing peace and harmony to the whole world.

AUGUST 28 -- PURPOSEFUL -- I am purposeful. Our Father's love is enfolding in us as peace. Peace is united with our purpose. We will not accept true peace without exploring our purpose. We have a part to play and place to be in the scheme of things. We are integral to creation and our purpose is the working of our part. See that it is our purpose to extend love and forgiveness to all whom we meet. We give love as we share our gifts with others, and as a result we receive many gifts in return. So, today, let us be purposeful in all that we do. Peace and prosperity come to us as a direct result of acting in the world with purpose. We have a place in God that no one else can fill...we have a combination of talents and abilities that are given to us in trust. Our purpose is to lovingly polish and hone these gifts...and then to give them away.

AUGUST 29 -- MISSIONARY -- I am on a mission. Our mission is a daily application of our purpose. As the day unfolds, we look for ways to be of service. Our mission is to be helpful at every opportunity. In this way we experience God's love by sharing it with our fellows. As we greet the new day we do so with an eye toward service. We lovingly contribute to our household, perhaps performing a task that is generally done by someone else. As we move out into the world, we see that the others on the road are on their own missions and we bless them. We are in the flow of traffic and we can facilitate that flow. In the workplace we are able to give, in old ways and new. We do not need to trumpet our beliefs to the world or try to convince anyone of anything. Our mission is simply to give service as we go through our ordinary day.

AUGUST 30 -- DIRECTION -- I am focused. Today, we will look to our greater goal: our total forgiveness of the world of conflict. Sight will clear as we become aware of the Love that surrounds us. We will know that everything we have need of in our pursuit is already provided, we will let go of any fear of what negative thing might occur and give our full effort to the goal we desire. We put our attention where we want to go, not on where we don't want to end up. We have learned the secret of direction. What we focus on grows, where we put our vision is the path that our feet will follow. Let us be single minded in our pursuit of mission and purpose. By focusing on what I want to accomplish, the way is made for us to achieve and succeed. Our vision points us to what we really want.

AUGUST 31 -- CONNECTION -- I am connected to Gods will. Gods will is for good. We are connected to this Goodwill and suffering is not part of It. Many times we may have wished and hoped for some good thing to come us. We may have prayed, begging or even demanding that God deliver the good(s). Today let us know that we are connected to all of the Good that the universe has for us. It is not something we have to long for; peace is something we just have to accept. This connection to All Good is our link to all the good that we need. Supply is flowing to us through the conduit of Gods love.

SEPTEMBER 1 -- ENERGIZED -- I am energized. Forgiving the appearance of lack provides more than enough of whatever we need to carry us through the day. Peace and prosperity come to us from the correct use of strength. Prosperity, is, of course, just one of the various forms that the energy takes, but it comes from the extension of strength down a course of action. As we forgive the world with the strength of divine energy, the gifts transform and reform and transform again and are then returned to us as still greater good. This process is an ongoing and continuous creation of supply. We extend love and we are extended to, in kind. Sometimes we may feel tired of all the effort, but we know that deep down within us there is more than enough energy, an unlimited supply of energy that will come to us as needed. We have the strength to forgive, which will deliver us all from the pain of separation.

SEPTEMBER 2 -- ENTHUSIASTIC -- I am alive, alert, awake, and enthusiastic. We are unlimited because in Spirit there is no limitation. We are alive with the life of God. Let us remain alert to all of the interactions of creation around me. We are awake to all of the possibilities of this day. Let us be enthusiastic about the day. Put attention on being a living expression of spirit. Share the intelligence and wisdom of the universe. All things are made new again, as we stay receptive to that guidance. Today, we see clearly in the light. We are no longer trapped in the shadows of self-centeredness. We are free to live and love in the light of God.

SEPTEMBER 3 -- TRUTH -- I am awakened to the truth. The truth is that we are all one. All other people are part of our family…they are truly brothers…sisters in spirit. All living things are part of our family; we are all linked in the life of God. Today, knowing that we cannot be apart from our brothers, we ask the Holy Spirit to guide us in all my interactions with others. This interaction is more than kind words; it is an ongoing work of service. We are now aware that we cannot truly prosper at the expense of anyone else. Our abundance and theirs is truly one. As we give to others, we receive in abundance. We love all of God's creations, seeing that we are all one family. Let us bless and encourage all forms of life that come into my life. Divine love shines in us and from us, giving radiance to the world. We are one with all life.

SEPTEMBER 4 -- SERVICE -- I am serving. A fulfilled life is a life of service. Today will be a day of conscious service. We will make a priority of being helpful. Any and every person we meet can be the recipient of our goodwill. Every task, every situation, every challenge will offer an opportunity to serve. So, what will we do, it is really very simple we will do what we always do. We go to work, to school, to the gym, to wherever we normally go; we do the things we normally do but with one difference. Today we will simply remember that every moment can be a moment of happiness if we make the choice to be helpful. We can serve others and we can serve ourselves in that same moment, extending love to our brothers and sisters results in love extending to ourselves.

SEPTEMBER 5 - CREATION -- I am co-creator with God. As I go about my life today, I want to be aware that I am constantly using my God-given talents. I am continually creating my experience. I can help create abundance or I can help make lack. God has already provided all of the possibilities for my prosperity, all I have to do is focus on selection. Spirit is continually guiding me in how to extend love out into my world. Spirit fills me with love, light and life...the keys to receiving all prosperity. I am intimately attuned to the activity of all creation...the continuing extension of the kingdom of God. I am an instrument of creation and I bless all those who come into contact with me, this day. I am looking for new ways to extend the kingdom in all that I do...co-creating the richness of life.

SEPTEMBER 6 - EXUBERANCE -- I am exuberant in my purpose. Hearing the voice for God, I remember my purpose and my peace are so intimately connected that they cannot stand apart. My job is to be of true service, giving love where it is needed and receiving love as a result. My purpose is to create. My mission is to be creative in every situation that appears before me today. I approach mission and purpose with exuberance. I am zealous in how I carry out all the things that need doing. There is an overflowing energy, which empowers me to achieve my aims. There is an all-powerful inspiration that leads me to do the right thing for the right reason at exactly the right time. Divine guidance increases as the day goes on, fueling my exuberance moment by moment.

SEPTEMBER 7 -- EXCITEMENT -- I am excited about life. My life is a continual enfoldment of joy. I can hardly wait to see what is going to happen next! My excitement fuels my daily activity. I know that there is peace in me that is stronger than any circumstance, or situation that may occur. This peace is generated directly from the presence of God within me. It is stronger than any need that might occur. I turn to this power throughout the day. I never knew that peace and excitement could exist together, but I know it now. I am on an adventure of a lifetime…everyday there is opportunity for great things. It is my attitude about it as well as my aptitude for it that will determine the outcome. I choose to maintain an attitude of gratitude and this fills me with the aptitude to make things happen. I know that everything that occurs today is part of this grand adventure in creation that I am a part of, and that is exciting.

SEPTEMBER 8 -- EXPECTATION -- I am expecting the best. Today I will expect to find God. I release my expectations of people, letting them be. I have changed my expectations. Whereas in the past I may have had a worried outlook for the future, I now have assurance that I am participating in abundance. I am in sacred communion with God. I expect all of my needs will be met in the right time and in the right way. I am grounded in my faith in God as my source and the source of all good. I expect prosperity and plenty. I expect perfect health...my mind is alert and my body is filled with power. The Divine life is moving in and through me...healing and revitalizing each and every cell. Divine intelligence is moving in and through me...inspiring my every thought. Divine power is moving in and through me...energizing my every action. I am one with God, the source of all blessings and I expect to be continually blessed. I expect the best and my expectations are always being bettered by the reality of life.

SEPTEMBER 9 - LIGHT -- I am well lit. The light of Christ is in me. As a direct result of applying love in my living, a great light has grown in me. It is the light of Christ, the image and likeness of God…God expressing himself as the essence of me. The light of Christ is my perfect self. It is the generated power of creation, it moves through me as a terrific energy. I have surrendered to the Christ, found faith in Its power, and aligned my will with Goodwill. I am judging rightly, examining myself and all others in Gods wisdom, and being open in my sharing of what I find. I operate out of divine order, putting first things first…and eliminating the negative. I understand my responsibility for life and am able to love and forgive everyone. I am stayed in this moment, allowing the presence and power of the Christ to guide me in my actions. I am whole and at one, awake and fully aware of the power within me and the presence that is all around me. The light of Christ is in me; the light of Christ is I.

SEPTEMBER 10 - UNITED -- I am in the Christ that unites us all. The Christ light is in me and it is in all others. My striving is to reach that place of Unity, where I see the light within all people. The light of God is shining forth from everyone. It is this truth that gives me the ability to interact in a positive way with everyone I meet. I am the light of love and wisdom in everyone. The light in me shines forth to facilitate harmony and peace in all my relationships. I radiate an optimistic attitude and an unfailing love for all Gods children. My day is made brighter as I focus on following the light that unites us all in God.

SEPTEMBER 11 - ACCEPTANCE -- I am non-judgmental. I accept people as they are. Today, I can accept everyone as they are; because I know that who they are is son/daughter of God…just like me. I see that all of my indictments…keep us all trapped in the illusion of sin. I hereby release all negative judgments of others. I hold all others and myself guiltless. I allow everyone to be him or herself without trying to force change. I do not try to impede the actions or desires of anyone. In the past it may have seemed important that other people act in certain ways, or that they do the things that I thought they should do. No more! I am content to be whom I am and I am content that others find their own path also.

SEPTEMBER 17 - FOCUS -- I am focused. I am focused on what is important and I do not let anything distract me from what is important. I put God first, and by doing that I remind myself that I am still in Him. Today, I have the principles and values of love, which are essential to my ongoing wellbeing. Love shifts my vision so that I will not let smaller ego issues shift my attention. I know that my good is tied to the good of others. I do not try to profit at the expense of others and I know that no one can take my good from me. I am focused on the extension of love and forgiveness.

SEPTEMBER 18 - SHARE -- I am sharing. I am safe in God, so I am not afraid to contribute my share to life. I share my good fortune and myself with the world. I am aware that I am continually receiving my good from Creation, and that it is my responsibility to give back to Creation. This responsibility is really just the knowledge that as I give I complete the cycle, which just starts another. Like my breath in which I receive and give life over and over again, I receive and I give all good over and over again. I contribute, doing what is mine to do with a sense of gratitude and honor. I am thrilled to be able to give to others and to contribute to the living of others. My share is the generosity that grows from my gratitude.

SEPTEMBER 19 - EXTENSION -- I am extending to others. There is no real difference between my fellows and I. Temporarily we may seem to have separate gifts but really we are all extending to each other. I am a veritable power plant of energy. I give this energy freely and I am continually recharging my batteries through the return flow from creation. I am part of God, and therefore very holy. I am responsible to share this energy with others. I make it my business to extend this holiness out from me to embrace each person and every situation that I come into contact with today. I can visualize an aura of sacred love emanating from me. This aura envelops everyone whom I meet. Anytime I encounter fear or uncertainty, I send my holiness forth to embrace the seeming difficulty. I marvel at how this power neutralizes fear and brings love into my world. I am an extension of God's love and I am determined to extend it out to the rest of the universe.

SEPTEMBER 20 - SHINE -- I am shining. My vision shows me my own true identity. I am the light on the side of the hill. I will not hide my light; I will not hinder my shining. I am committed to be a beacon for others to follow. I am not embarrassed or ashamed of whom I am. I feel the light of Christ shining from me. I will be the genuine article, no more hiding or acting, genuine and true to myself. As I allow myself to be unguarded and open, I am able to see past the limitations of personality in myself and in others...I can see what is really here. Throughout the day I get to the meat of the matter...I discern the underlying principle and work easily with it. I shine, and my shining effects activate the brilliance of everyone that I come into contact with.

SEPTEMBER 21 – GIFT -- I am a gift. Everyone who comes to me this day is a gift. God gives the best to me. Although sometimes I don't see it, Spirit is always offering miracles. However I perceive the world, only the Love of God is real. Grace blesses me at all times and in all places. Today, I look for signs of goodwill. I see the world as a symbol for creation rather than destruction. I will accept my wellbeing with faith in its ultimate benefit. I know that I will receive whatever it is that I request. I just need request what I really want. Releasing guilt, I am worthy of happiness. Releasing judgment, I am aligned with wisdom. Releasing fear, I am filled with love. I remember that I am never alone…I see the gift of God everywhere.

SEPTEMBER 22– GRATITUDE -- I am giving. I give the best to God. I am so grateful for my gifts. Today, I will give my best to God, I will give my best to everyone I meet and in all situations in which I find myself. I will release all thought of sacrifice or lack. I will look at all of my work as play in which I am delighted. I will see all of my efforts to help others as free gifts, given with only the joy of giving as my motive. I know that when I give freely, more gifts freely flow to me. It is a joy to give my best, my best at home, my best in the workplace, and my best in the community. The good that is in me wants to express through me and today I will allow it. I am free of all suffering whenever I am intent on being and giving my best.

SEPTEMBER 23 - FEARLESS -- I am forgiving. I forgive all fear. We are the holy Son of God. Spirit smiles on us with love and tenderness, deep and dear. The universe smiles back to itself remembering it shares holiness with us. All of the love of God is bestowed upon us. Brotherhood and Fatherhood are one and complete. Together, we are without sin and perfect in the eyes of God. Therefore, let us forgive all fear, for if God sees it not, how can it be real. There are only two states in our minds, love and fear.... and fear is just a lie we tell ourselves. God made us whole and without sin (read fear). In whole sinless-ness then we remember Meister Eckhart's words "We are all Words of God, books about God." As we observe the world we forgive all that is not Good.

SEPTEMBER 24 -- MERCY -- I am protected. God asks
no sacrifice. We are not asked to any sacrifice to find mercy.
No sacrifice is needed for peace. The mercy and peace of
God are free. To believe that God expects something of us
is to forget that He is already the all of us. He does not have
to expect, He knows. He knows us as Son; he extends all
goodness to us as a result. The only cost to Salvation is that
it be freely given and received; by definition then it cannot
be purchased. Our practice then for today is to accept the
mercy that is always present. We receive the gifts of God and
without any worry whatsoever we extend them out to others.
We cannot lose by giving because God asks no sacrifice.

SEPTEMBER 25 - LAW --- I am loving. I give love to all, and it becomes my gift to myself. The law of giving and receiving is ancient and true. Whatever we give will be our own reward. Sometimes we lose track of true value. We may believe that by giving, we are reduced by that amount. Today, let us turn those false thoughts aside. Let us stop withholding the good and let us stop giving the negative. Our gift to our brother is indeed our gift to ourselves. If we make a present of peace and extend it out, it returns to us. Extend a blessing and be blessed. To have love, give love. To have time, give time. To have treasures, give treasures. We remember that to have all we give all to all. The law of love is that it is all there is, therefore it is all that we are. All that we have to give is the love that is us.

SEPTEMBER 26- FORTUNE -- I am fortunate. I extend good fortune. The goodness of the universe is extending to us at all times. The good in our lives is a reflection of miracles. We are son and heir to God. The law of love is universal and today we continue to practice it. Even in the midst of seeming chaos and conflict the law of giving and receiving is apparent. If we give from our fear, fear increases. If we give from peace we become a center of peace. When we invest ourselves in life the dividends are great. We feel the connections, we relate to all living things as we gratefully give ourselves to them. Our fortune is great indeed when we see that it is life itself!

SEPTEMBER 27 - ENVELOPED -- I am enveloped. The peace of God envelops me. Today, let's awaken to the truth. There is nothing but God. We are always in the midst of the divine. To realize this is to find the peace that passeth all understanding. Think about how simple this idea is...we are always and forever one with the Source. We are enveloped in the light of Gods love. We rest in this love, we relax into this presence and we remember nothing but the peace of God. As awareness of this peace grows in us, we become a center of peace for others. We come to understand that our own well-being depends on us giving peace to those around us. It is so natural and happens with such ease that it is not a burden. The peace of God envelops us and it is our joy to extend the envelope to all of those whom we meet.

SEPTEMBER 28 -- TASKED -- I am tasked. I have a task and I need to see my work through the eyes of Spirit. Wherever we find ourselves, we have a task. Some thing to do, some gift to give...wherever...whenever we are. We are here to be helpful and as we have read: "truly helpful". Being truly helpful means being attuned to the Christ and operating out of God's will. Sometimes we may get caught up in trying to figure out what we should do. This is a waste of time and energy. If we get quiet and ask for guidance we will be guided. It will become apparent what to do and when to do it.

SEPTEMBER 29 -- AUTHORITY -- I am surrendered. I surrender only to the authority of God. Take a moment right now to surrender all illusions of individual existence. Just relax, let the presence of a loving God become apparent to you. Yes, it's right there, so close, and now you are in the presence and the presence is in you. The light of God is available to you at all times and in all places. When you surrender to it, the focus of the moment becomes the authority of the your Father. From this place it is clear what needs to be done.

SEPTEMBER 30 -- INSPIRED -- I am inspired. God speaks through others to me and to others through me. This doesn't just happen automatically, first we must ask Spirit to allow us to hear what we need to hear and then to guide us in what we need to say. As we practice the presence, God is able to speak through us. Feel yourself releasing the ego. Set aside all of the insane babble of thoughts, if only just for a moment. The voice for God is speaking right now. The words of spirit are like cool water to the thirsty. They uplift us and inspire us. If we can maintain this state of mind, all that proceeds from us will be goodwill. God will speak through us, through our words and our actions.

OCTOBER 1 – EQUABLE -- I am free from extremes. I allow all unpleasantness to fall away. Today, I follow the middle way. I let go of past patterns, establishing myself in the present. I am neither attached to material things, nor do I reject them. I do not pursue or avoid. I enjoy the good that has shown up in the world of form. I am able to take pleasure in things without letting them control me. I am surrounded by beauty and I am able to appreciate it without having to own it. I am active in mind and body, but I also know when to rest. I am centered in the presence of God.

OCTOBER 2 – EQUALITY -- I am connected. I value my brother. My brother and I are one. All of his gifts are given to me and all of mine are given him. All other people are part of my family…we are truly brothers in spirit. All living things are part of my family; we are all linked in the life of God. Today, knowing that I cannot be apart from my brothers, I ask the Holy Spirit to guide me in all my interactions with others. This interaction is more than kind words; it is an ongoing work of service. I am aware that I cannot truly prosper at the expense of anyone else. My abundance and theirs is truly one. As I give to others, I receive in abundance. I love all of God's creations, seeing that we are all one family. I bless and encourage all forms of life that come into my life. Divine love shines in me and from me, giving radiance to the world. I am one with all life.

OCTOBER 3– EQUANIMITY -- I am calm. I forgive all of my anger. I give the gift of forgiveness. I am tired of seeing my life through the filter of the past. Calmness and peace fill me as I let go of the past. I am innocent and hold no grievance against myself or anyone else. I trust the ever-expanding possibilities in life. Anger fades as I see myself integrated into life. I am an equal in creation. I have so much peace because I know that I cannot be threatened. As Son of God, I am protected and provided for at all times. Therefore, I am calm and serene. I view my day and my life with tranquility.

OCTOBER 4– EQUAL -- I am equal. I treat everyone as equal. Today I see reality, that everything is part of God. Everyone is a child of God. This reality reminds me that although I am special and unique so is everyone else. The only way this can be is if everyone else is too. I see all of the people that I come into contact with as my brothers (and sisters) in God. We are all irreplaceable parts of the cosmos. Each of us has a place and a part in the unfolding of the universe. My way is the way of equality and harmony…I will follow that way. Today I see that everyone is a perfect child of God, regardless of his or her behavior.

OCTOBER 5 – CAPABILITY -- I am capable of doing what is called for. I am equal to the task at hand. I am strong in the light of God; I bring safety to any who cross my path. Sometimes I may feel that something is keeping me in place, keeping me from accomplishing what I desire. Today, I know that I am capable of overcoming whatever obstacle in my path. I take responsibility for my life and I know that I can soar to new heights by releasing past hurts and regrets. I let go of all guilt and remorse…I forgive all resentments. I can learn from the past, but I can also rise above it. Realizing my oneness with the Divine, I "lighten" up. My mind and heart are cleansed and I move out and up! The very life and light of God are within me, lifting me on high, and I am strong and capable in it.

OCTOBER 6 – EQUATION -- I am in balance. My life is balanced. Body, mind and spirit are balanced in me. I am in harmony with others. I bring body and mind into harmony, which in turn brings harmony into all relationships. I give myself over to the power of God in me and in doing so I realize I can do whatever is called for. I am goodwill in action, as I perceive myself and all others in Light. I open myself to Life and to divine order. I release all disease in my mind and body. The strength of God flows through me allowing forgiveness. I am focused in and centered on this moment. My vision is single and I am full of energy to compete all of my tasks this day. I am in harmony with God, and therefore I am in harmony with all others. My life is one; all of the aspects of who I am are balanced and harmonious.

OCTOBER 7 -- SERVICE -- I am a servant. "...And the greatest among you will be your servants." This is a wonderful reference to the power of service. A fulfilled life is a life of service. Awake to the fact that we are not alone, aware of the value of our fellows and sensing our connection to all life we go forth and perform simple acts of helpfulness. Today, we are free from pain. Free to experience all of the opportunities for good that present themselves to us. We watch for chances to give love in all situations. Because we now know that our role in life is to be a facilitator we also understand that our happiness is also linked to our facilitation. As we continue to help we will be helped, as we extend ourselves to life we will be extended to, and as we love we will be loved. Actually this love is always present and it is through our giving it that we become aware of Love's presence.

OCTOBER 8 -- INTEGRITY – I am true to my values. I show respect to all those in my life. I am committed to speak only positive words, which build up and bind together. I am one with the Father in my pursuit of creative living. I will extend new life and new love today. I know that I have absolutely nothing to fear, so I am transparent in all my dealings. People sense that I am at peace and they are drawn to me. The love of God showers me this day, and I can afford to sprinkle a little of that love on the ones who will cross my path. In fact when I focus on loving, even more love comes to me. So, I give a little more and then even more, as I become a veritable fountain of God's love. Following this path I become a magnet, drawing all those people who thirst for this water of life.

OCTOBER 9 -- PRINCIPLE --- I am principle in action. There is nothing that can separate me from the Good that God has for me. I am the herald of the coming of the Lord. This is not some superstition. God is trying to act through each of us everyday. Today I will pay attention to this guidance. I bring my attention to the Truth, focusing on principles. I am not on this path by chance. I have divine appointments to keep. My personality cannot keep me from my mission and the personalities of others cannot distract me from my purpose. I will keep my thoughts centered on God; and God will keep me centered in principle. I will continue on my journey giving and receiving blessings as I go. My life is a pillar built on the rock of principle and I see that my life joined with the lives of others is helping to support many good things.

OCTOBER 10 – PRESENCE – I am in the presence. God is all there is. As I become quiet and centered in prayer, I am deeply aware of the presence of God within me. This awareness of God within me is just the beginning. As I focus, I begin to notice the presence in others; looking more intently I see that this presence is everywhere in everyone and in everything. With continued practice I see God in situations and circumstances. I no longer feel that I am at the mercy of chance events. There is a holy aura about and around people regardless of how they act. The world is becoming more and more beautiful. I am filled with spirit. I am caught up in the magnificence of all these symbols of the ultimate glory of God. I look with new eyes, I hear with new ears. I am connected to life in uncountable ways. I rejoice in the oneness of all things. I know that God is all there is.

OCTOBER 11 – FORWARD --- I am in the flow of life. All religions are like streams that lead to the ocean of God. Rumi says: "All religions, all this singing, is one song. The differences are just illusion and vanity. The sun's light looks a little different on this wall than it does on that wall... but it's still one light." Today, I will sing a new song; today I will sing a song of one-ness. I will release my old ways of thinking. I become humble and able to be open-minded. I know that the light of God is not just coming from the sun but is also shining out from the eyes of those around me and from all living things. I am not threatened by the beliefs of others. I can disagree without being disagreeable. I understand that in faith no one is wrong. I see all paths lead to God; all these religions are indeed streams flowing into the ocean of Creation...

OCTOBER 12 – GOOD --- I am good. My body, mind and spirit are all good. The energy of Creation is the energy which makes up my body, it is the energy that sparks my mind and it is the energy that enlivens my spirit. I know that the body is neutral and will respond to goodwill. In this way is my body made healthy and all of its functions made holy. Today, I sanctify my body. My mind is alert and responsive, it is connected to the mind of God, and as such it is always receiving holy thoughts. I choose to focus on these holy thoughts, releasing any negativity. Knowing that I am all good, my spirit soars, it is caught up in the joy of creation, and it flies with angels. My body, mind and spirit are in harmony. I bring peace, wisdom and love together in me. God abides in the midst of me; today I focus on that. The first thing I notice is that my body is relaxed and at peace. My mind begins to reflect the wisdom of divine mind. My spirit revels in the love of God. Peace, wisdom and love come together in me, so that my body, mind and spirit are in harmony.

OCTOBER 13 – HARMONIOUS --- I am in harmony. My personal life, business life and social life are in harmony. As I start a new day concerns about life may seem almost overwhelming. I remember that I can find peace if I turn my attention to God. I relax, release and let go right now. I focus on my breath, breathing in the presence of God and breathing out the power of God. Soon I am uplifted and energized. God is always there, just waiting for me to notice. From this calm place I am able to see that everything is in divine order. I put first things first, getting my good characteristics in front of my personality. In my dealings with others today I am kind and responsive. I follow my inner guide and everything flows together in an efficient way. My life is in harmony; all things are working together for good. I am one with the Creator and I am creating a wonderful life experience.

OCTOBER 14 – PRAYER --- I am connected to creation through prayer. Today, I continue my practice of prayer. I pray for others, binding us all in love. Love is the ability to feel connected to and desiring only good to come to all others. Today, I reaffirm my love. I give only good thoughts to my loved ones. I affirm that they will experience the presence of God in all that they do. I see this presence caring for them, going with them where I cannot go. The love of God heals them and makes them whole. I know that they can overcome any challenge through the light of God in them. I extend this Light in all of my prayers.

OCTOBER 15 --- RATIONAL --- I am rational. Today I will focus my mind in a way that encourages rational thought. Critical thinking is rational thinking. I do not just accept what I am being told as true. I examine things in the light of logic and the understanding of my heart. I am not a prisoner of past prejudices; I am free of the ill taught lessons of upbringing and environment. I release all superstition. I am not ignorant. I know that how I see the world is just a reflection of what is present in my mind. I understand the difference between spiritual things and the belief in magic. I know that seeming evil is just the misapplication of creative power, not the tool of some malevolent force. I know that I am capable of "evil" but that I am not trapped in it. I can decide to work for good and release all superstition. I am rational and I will see the world in that light.

OCTOBER 16 --- UNIFIED --- I am coming together. My being is integrated and balanced. My mind and body are one. The twin hemispheres of my brain are now united. My intellect and my intuition are wed. Humility, knowing who I am and not trying to act like something else, is the antidote to vanity. Vanity has been telling me alternately that I am less than some and more than others…it is a lie… all are of equal value to the universe. I am of two minds no longer; my being is healed and whole. My male and female natures have come together and are working in harmony to create an attitude of justice and equality…right judgment and compassion. The Father and the Mother have become one in me and in that union a new world is born.

OCTOBER 17 --- HARMONY --- I am in harmony with others. I bring body and mind into harmony, which in turn brings harmony into all relationships. I give myself over to the presence of God in me and in doing so I realize oneness with creation. I am goodwill in action, as I perceive myself and all others in Light. I open myself to Life and to divine order. I release all disease in my mind and body. The strength of God flows through me allowing forgiveness. I am focused in and centered on this moment. My vision is single and I am full of energy to complete all of tasks this day. I am in harmony with God, and therefore I am in harmony with all others.

OCTOBER 18--- EXTENSION --- I am extending. I extend the light of love to everyone. I visualize the light in my heart moving through my body and then extending out from me to touch everyone. I am an extension of Creation and I extend myself in a like manner. I give to the universe and the universe gives to me. I understand that everything I do is an extension of Creation. I am deeply involved in the unfolding good of the universe. My presence is the harbinger of good things for everyone around me. I am fully conscious of my ability to extend light and enfold the person in front of me, as well as any room that I may enter or the building where I work, or even the entire world.

OCTOBER 19 --- CONNECTION --- I am connected to those who came before. Today as I remember my forbearers I am filled with courage and energy. I have genetic ancestors, a line of life that extends back into the mists of time; these are my predecessors, those who prepared the way for me. I can honor them in my memory and in my moment-to-moment living. Their spirit, part of all spirit is eternal, just like mine, so they are really still available to me. I also have other forbearers, mentors, historical figures who have inspired me, and anyone else who helped me develop into who I am today. I honor them also. I realize that we are all part of the great web of life that is not limited in time and space. I honor all of those who came before, when I remember them and then act in a manner that reflects favorably on their teachings. I am connected to those who came before.

OCTOBER 20 --- BRIDGE --- I am the bridge for those yet to come. Just as I am still one with those who preceded me, I span the present to the future for those yet to come. I am conscious of the fact that I am role model to the young. I am aware that the acts of today impact tomorrow. I pay attention to my words and actions so that they can be a positive example. Just as my ancestors and those who inspired me were a bridge from their time to mine, I am likewise for those who come after. This is both honor and responsibility. To help keep the planet intact, to contribute to the growing store of knowledge, to stand for freedom and equality, to extend love and teach harmony…all of these are a rich inheritance. I intend to will all of these things to the future, for I am the bridge for those yet to come.

OCTOBER 21--- HAPPY --- I am happy. I am happy for the good fortune of others. Any time that I may be jealous of another's good fortune; I stop and change my mind. I understand that by begrudging the good of others, I block my own. Today, I celebrate the good that comes to us all. I bless others and I become a blessing to others. If I see success happening for someone, I emulate them. I look for ways that I can learn from their example. Today, I turn envy into blessings, I know that when I acknowledge that my brother deserves the good that comes to him that I am also opening the way for my own good to come to me. So, I am happy...I celebrate the good fortune of others.

OCTOBER 22 - TOLERANT - I am tolerant. We are tolerant of each other. Judgment pulls us into a world of conflict. It makes us superior or inferior in our mind, which just leads to further separation from our brothers and sisters. It occurs through self-centeredness, it is the avoidance of our own subconscious guilt by applying it to others. Our honesty reminds us that we are all in this together and each of us is capable of any of these bad acts that we judge others for. We only lie to ourselves when we see others as apart from us. Trust builds tolerance and honesty demands it. So, today let us accept everyone, as they are; in noticing their error we can regard our own and then move quickly to seeing through to the truth of the divine in others and ourselves. Acceptance of divinity in us all leads to gratitude and peace. Notice that as we apply this principle today our learning grows. Today, our perception will move a great distance toward our goal.

OCTOBER 23 - GENTLE - I am gentle. To be gentle, to be harmless, that is our focus today. Because love does not oppose, neither do we; because love cannot be opposed, neither are we. There is no call for harm, because it is a fruitless effort, which just reinforces our ties to the ego. We will call for no punishment for others and we will accept none for ourselves. There is a quiet confidence in us that arises from our reliance on the strength of Spirit. Our path to heaven runs through gentleness and this attribute comes directly out of our inner strength. We let go of fear and embrace love, which neutralizes all enmity. Any impulse to do otherwise can be healed by giving it to Spirit. Gently now, we align our will with Goodwill and throughout the day we will experience that Will.

OCTOBER 24 - JOY - I am joyous. Our gentleness has led us to joy. Fear is released and joy floods in to take its place. We open our hands and our hearts to those around us in a grateful sharing of what we have found. No words are really necessary unless we are guided to say something uplifting. All of our pain is forgotten, all suffering fades in the light of our joy. As we gently move through this day we are attended by profound happiness. We will notice no attack as we place the gifts of Love before each one, and receive those same as well. In our hearts a quiet refrain of peace and joy is heard. We will do well to extend this happy melody out to the world we see, and notice its effect.

OCTOBER 25 - DEFENSE - I am defenseless. We are taught to be defenseless. Living simply, we let go of the need to acquire. When material things come to us, we gratefully make use of them and then when we need them no more we let them go. God has made us perfect in Spirit and there is no need for us to try make something better for ourselves in the world. This does not mean that we do not have work to do, it does not mean that we should not endeavor to achieve, it just means that we need to remember our goal of God in all that we do. A deep understanding has settled upon us now...we know that we are God's own and there is great comfort in that. And if we are of God then who or what shall we fear? God does not need defense...and as his, neither do we. Our true safety lies in our defenselessness. Offense and defense are two sides of the same coin that continues to spend itself on misery. Let go of the guards, release the chains, and unlock the gates. Spirit protects us now and always. As we lay down our arms we are protected in much stronger ones.

OCTOBER 26 - GENEROSITY - I am generous. We can only keep what we have by giving it away. This seems to fly in the face of worldly thinking. Obviously if I have a certain thing and then I give this thing away I will not have it anymore. The gifts of Spirit however can never be lost. When we truly give of ourselves we receive all that we give and more. "To have all give all to all." This is a quote from the workbook of A Course in Miracles, which has been a cause for concern among many students. It is referring to the Gift of Self to Self. It is not concerned with the conditional gifts of the material world. This principle is the total relinquishment of our self into the whole of Life. We may ask where this leaves us concerning material things. Well first, the material is temporary and not any real value in and of itself, but we remember that all things in the world are just symbols. So, the ability to give what we have in the world is a talent we should reinforce. We could say that we should not accept gifts that we could not bear to turn around and give to someone else because then they would be a hindrance to our ongoing. Be generous and know that all things are provided.

OCTOBER 27 - PATIENCE - I am patient. We are patient. We can be patient when we know that Heaven is already ours. There is no anxiety or upset concerning the events of this day or any other because we are sure of the outcome... we will get where we are going. We can avoid delays in the world and get there a little quicker, we can learn to forgive and get back to Love a lot quicker. But make no mistake; all those detours and errors are forgiven and then made as if they never occurred. Patience is the companion of peace and the friend of calm. We can relax ourselves in perfect confidence that late or not we will get there, in the world and in Heaven. This means we can give ourselves a break, but it also means we must give others a break. Anyone who seems to be getting in the way of our goal is just another opportunity for forgiveness and a teaching/learning experience. Be patient with us, We are not done with us yet!

OCTOBER 28 - FAITHFUL - I am faithful. We are faithful. The power of faith is our perceiving power...it is the medium in which we see. Belief is part of it, but also the assurance that in Reality all is well. True faithfulness gives all things to the care of God. This is hard at first, we may feel comfortable turning over certain problems that seem out of our ability to fix but then hold on to the situations that we think we are in control of. We may be willing to give some relationships but not others; we may relinquish some past events but continue to resent or regret selected memories. Fear is keeping us from realizing the Power of faith...we are afraid that letting go of some specific issues will end in outcomes that we do not want. Right now let us get quiet and examine our readiness. Being entirely ready to have God remove some things but not others is really not being entirely ready. Do not despair this! Even a small amount of readiness will begin the process...as we begin to give our fears to Spirit we learn that the outcome is peace and we become more willing to release other things. In this way our faith will grow... so start today, allow faith to replace fear in some area and just notice how belief and assurance grow.

OCTOBER 29 - CERTAIN - I am certain. Today's idea may just be a hopeful affirmation, but we can know that it is the outcome of continued practice. We will from time to time deviate from our path, this is just a temporary delay. Our faith is a rock of certainty. Deep within us is absolute certainty; today let us endeavor to reach it. In quiet we allow our consciousness to focus on what is on the inside. For a time let us release the reflections and shadows of the world; we look to the true light that gleams in us. See it now, as it shines forth from our center. All distractions are left behind as we become more and more aware of our true identity. All of the worldly things that we have been focused on are now of no concern. In the light we know that we are cared for and we are caring...without fear we are able to just be. There is no need, no lack, and no danger. We exist in God and there is nothing in God that would harm us in any way. Here we are certain, certain of the Love that sustains us and certain that we can extend that Love to wash away any seeming conflict in our lives.

OCTOBER 30 - CONSISTENT - I am consistent. We are consistent. When we are honest about who our brother is we establish an honest view of ourselves. Both (all) of us precious in God, equal in Spirit...One with each other. Once this honesty is established we can be consistent in our dealings with everyone and in every situation. Visualize it now. See that we are so comfortable in our Unity that we do not need to treat anyone as "less than or more than" all of us equal and all of us deserving of the Love of God. Being consistent means that we act in the same manner in every situation. Here lies our direction for today and everyday, in every instance give fear to Spirit and then receive gentleness in is place. Based on this simple model we can increase consistency without effort, because we realize that it is the gift of the Holy Spirit. Every worry given to Him will be changed to joy and the ability to extend that joy out into our perceived world will be given back to us.

OCTOBER 31 - CONFIDENT - I am confident. Confidence is not arrogance. Confidence is not aggression. Confidence does not force its will on anyone. True confidence arises from our inner strength, which is a totally non-threatening power. It is quiet and unassuming; it does not need to show itself in braggadocio. Confidence does not need to change others; it is tolerant exactly because it is comfortable with itself. Today, let us allow this attribute to come forth from us as an aid in all that we need to do. We are able to begin any task knowing that the Holy Spirit goes with us; we are able to stay focused on our mission even in the face of distraction. Every temptation is laid aside by relying on Our strength. At peace, calm and assured we move out into the world with our confidence allowing us to accomplish that which is ours to do this day. We are attractive and inviting to those around us, some of who will seek our help. Our efforts are graceful and kind, and relying on our strength we are able to see every task complete.

NOVEMBER 1 - OPEN-MINDED - I am open-minded. We are open-minded. Today we will attempt release...as we relax into our breath we are reminded of the flow of life. We are receiving and we are giving. The breath becomes our symbol for living; on the in-breath we receive, on the out-breath we give. We open our hands to accept the good that comes and we leave them open to return the favor. We open our heart to the inflowing of love and let it remain open so that love can flow back out. We open our minds to the inspiration of Spirit and we allow that inspiration to extend out from our mind into our actions in the world. Being open-minded means that we can release the old, limiting ideas from the past and be ready to accept the solution to any seeming difficulty. Open-minded we allow preconceptions to be erased and replaced by the present moment. Open-minded we are ready to perform our function, which is to say "observe the face of Christ in all things".

NOVEMBER 2 -- BEING -- God is. God is in all, all is in God. We share one Being, which is God. Take a moment to consider the all-ness of God. Think about the Big Bang in which the universe we know came into being. This explosion of being could not be observed from outside, there was no outside. This seminal event was the beginning of separation. It was actually the beginning of the "outside". It was the tiny mad idea that we could be apart from God. Before the Big Bang, God was, after the Big Bang, God is. Creation was and creation is one being, whole and integrated. This is the ultimate truth, a certainty that we cannot be separate from God, because there is nothing that exists apart from God.

NOVEMBER 3 -- BE -- I am. Today, let me remember that I am an extension of God. I will remember throughout the day to just be. I will be who and what I am without any concern for what others think or how they may react to my genuine presence. I will not worry about what I am supposed to do. I will not fret over who I am supposed to impress. I will simply be. I relax into the presence of Love, knowing that I will be gently led to do the things that are mine to do.

NOVEMBER 4 – QUIET – God is speaking. I am listening. Today, I will endeavor to be quiet. I will move through the day aware that God is speaking. I will pay attention to the still, soft voice within me. The words of God are all around me, beckoning me to hear. All of the living things are the words of God and they talk with the voice of God. I am so grateful that the word of God is not trapped, static, in some book. God is speaking…speaking life, right now and forever. God does not stop, nothing is finished or done. All things are proceeding from the mouth of God and they will continue to proceed…and I will continue to listen.

NOVEMBER 5 – OBSERVE -- I am observant. I am witness to life. As I watch, I see the wonder of creation unfolding all around me. Sometimes, my self-consciousness keeps me from noticing what is going on. The very thing that opens the way for humanity stops me from experiencing my humanness. Humanity is the very state of the Son-ship. As human we are able to move from the self-conscious fear state into the consciousness of Self as part of creation. So, today, I will release the old fears of partition and embrace the one-ness of God. I sit quietly, observing as the web of life is knit together moment by moment. I have an inner knowing that my observation affects that which is observed, so I watch with love.

NOVEMBER 6 – EXPANSION -- I am expanding. As learning in the world expands, consciousness increases. I am not afraid. My mind is open and receptive. I have no enemies, as I am one with creation. My destiny is one that choice dictates. I am protected because spirit cannot be destroyed. My values are of love; in whose true image I am made. I use the traditions of the past as guideposts along the way to the future. They are guides, but not dictators. I understand that the nature of the universe is change and so my experience changes with it; I also understand that the nature of spirit is unchanging so the essence of me never changes. I know that as the universe continues to expand so do I.

NOVEMBER 7 – REALITY -- I am real. God is the reality of life. God is not some judge-on-high who is continually keeping track of the ins and outs of our lives. God is life itself, the whole wonderful package. The messiness, the seeming chaos, the unknowable outcomes, God is in all of these and more. God is not manipulated by our prayers, but rather is the power that resides in them. God is not concerned about specifics, but is the spark of creation that exists in all of the details. God does not protect us physically, but continually holds our spirit unharmed. God does not ask us to be born again, but to remain new in each unfolding moment. God is not some old, lame myth but rather the vibrant life of the universe continually spilling God-self out in new and wondrous ways. This is reality, this is the reality of God.

NOVEMBER 8 – UNBOUND -- I am free. From the old Unity song, we hear "I am free, I am unlimited, there are no ties that bind me". Today, let us release all of the old bugaboos that would hold us to fear and uncertainty. As Son of God we are free to do and to be. We are free to cross the boundaries which seem to separate males from females. We are free to accept the outcast. We can enrich our own experience by opening the door to those who are now on the outside. We are free to forgive what we have been told is unforgivable...whatever that may be. We are not bound by the past, our own or anyone else's. We have never been properly served by rejecting those who seemed different... we just continued to affirm a difference that is really not present. We are part of the whole of humanity and the whole of creation itself...we are free from tribe, prejudice, gender, sexual orientation, religion, finitude and fear. We are free...

NOVEMBER 9 – PRESENT -- I am present in God. God is present in me. God is with(in) me. From Psalm 139: 7-12: "Whither shall I go from thy Spirit? Or whither shall I flee from thy presence? If I ascend to heaven, thou art there! If I make my bed in Sheol, thou art there! If I take wings of the morning and dwell in the uttermost parts of the sea, even there thy hand shall lead me, and thy right hand shall hold me. If I say, "Let only darkness cover me, and the light about me be night," even the darkness is not dark to thee, the night is bright as the day; for darkness is as light with thee." Here it is…a fantastic insight into the truth of the ever-present God. From earliest times, some knew what we now see…God is always with/within us. No matter where we go physically or mentally God is there. This is our ultimate comfort…

NOVEMBER 10 – PART -- I am (with)in God. I am part of God…and I have a part in God. I cannot be apart from Spirit because I am Spirit. My elder brother Jesus, sends me forth in Matthew (28:18-20) "All authority in heaven and on earth has been given to me. Go therefore and make disciples of all nations, baptizing them in the name of the Father and of Son and of the Holy Spirit, and teaching them to obey everything that I have commanded you. And remember, I am with you always, to the end of the age." Again the message of universality…follow the law and teach it to all you meet. The law is that love binds us to God and to each other. We show that we are with God and in God when we extend God as we move through our moments and our days. We carry the good news that all are one, that the Kingdom of Heaven is One, and that oneness is all there is.

NOVEMBER 11 – EXPRESSION – I am expressing. God loves and lives through us. God is the Ground of All Being. All things grow out of that ground. Not a being, but Being. To touch reality, we must learn to love in all circumstances. This is how God expresses through us, no other way but love. Jesus made it clear: "You have heard it said: Love your family and hate your enemy, but I say unto you: Love your enemy and do good to those who persecute you." This is the path to peace. Our expression of God will be as good as our ability to forgive. There is someone in your life that will activate this expression, and it is not the person you feel closest to. It is the one you feel alienated from. See them now, looking for your forgiveness, extending their own to you simultaneously. This is our shared salvation, the only one that is real. In this salvation, God loves and lives through us and as us.

NOVEMBER 12 -- GIFT -- I am gifted with prayer. Prayer is the means by which I return my consciousness to God-awareness. It is my soul singing to Creation. Take a moment right now to get the feel of this, prayer is thought and those thoughts are a song unto God. They can be harmonious or they can be dissonant. They can have order and pattern or they can be random and chaotic. The song that is sweet to the heavenly ear is one that exudes the love of which we are a part. So, the prayer which is grateful and joyous is the gift which derives from the original gift and then gives back to it. An attitude of good fortune will cause more to be grateful for. As I focus on the gift, being happy for it, the song of my heart produces a vibration which spills into my outer life in ways that cannot be fully explained or even predicted. So I am gifted and I am a gift.

NOVEMBER 13 -- GOAL -- I am releasing all goals but God. Today I see the futility of putting outer desires in front of my hearts desire to be one with God. It is not that I need to live some sort of monastic life, bereft of comfort. I just need to make unification with Life my primary goal. So I will focus my prayers (thoughts) on coming together with my brothers and sisters, knowing that this is essential to being at one with God. If I put first things first, if I put Relationship first, then everything else will get into divine order. I do not need to worry about not getting what I need, I can relax knowing that my Father already knows what I need and has provided it. All of the aspirations, the wants and needs that are in my best interest will be given when I am willing to accept them. By surrendering my will into Goodwill, I hasten the arrival of these good things into my life experience.

NOVEMBER 14 -- DREAMS -- I am letting go of ego dreams. We are Son of God; as such we inherit the Kingdom. This is the ultimate legacy, that which contains all of the Good in Creation. I do not need to fantasize about getting more stuff, more money, more attention, more approval or more of any other ego need. I am already complete...whole and healthy. My life is the very definition of abundance. It is only my wishing for what I think I lack that keeps me from realizing my inherent wealth. So today, let us release dreams of filling lack with more trinkets...let us instead turn our attention the rich nature of the universe. We can only receive our good when we are ready to accept it. By thinking that we don't have it we actually keep it from ourselves. There is no lack, all we have need of is already provided! As we affirm the presence of prosperity in us and all around us it will be made apparent in our lives.

NOVEMBER 15 -- REACH -- I am reaching for God. There is no cost for the attainment of one-ness. Truly the cost of denying it is great in suffering, but through prayer we are able to release the pain of separation and come into atonement. All prayer is answered. When we pray for things or particular outcomes the answers are various but usually unfulfilling and certainly not for the highest good. We can feel the presence of God right now just by asking Spirit to make it known. This presence is already provided and it is only our ego which blocks our awareness of It. Ego believes that if it allows the Presence to be felt, it would lose control. Well this is true...ego, which controls a pitiful and minuscule dark corner of our mind will fade into the light of universal consciousness once God is reached. This is an incalculably good exchange for us. We lose self-consciousness (self-centeredness) and gain God consciousness. Prayer allows us to connect with this condition (at least a shadow of it) for extended periods of time until we actually cross the threshold into the Kingdom eternally.

NOVEMBER 16 -- ANSWERS -- I am answered by the Holy Spirit. Sometimes we can't help it, even knowing that it is best just to ask for knowledge of God's will and the power to carry that out, we have to ask for specific answers to specific questions. We don't need to feel bad. Ask away! Holy Spirit will take our question and provide an answer that we can understand right now. Realize that whatever the problem of the moment seems to be, it is just a symbol...a shadow of the real problem (separation). It is perfectly fine to deal with this specifically and spirit will provide a specific answer for it. So we can ask for whatever it is we think we need, paying attention to the answer, knowing that we are being led to a greater understanding. Be grateful and give thanks that all questions will be answered at the right time and in the right way always for our shared benefit.

NOVEMBER 17 -- SONG -- I am hearing a song from heaven. In our meditations we are attempting to enter the realm of unity. There is a quiet place in us, where all conflict disappears and all problems find solution. A place of peace and harmony. The music that plays there is the sound of oneness. All dissonance resolves in a melody of loving kindness. Our hearts synchronize with the pulse of creation. The rhythms of life transport us to blissful awareness of the presence of God. An Echo of the holy Voice brings lyrics that remind of us of who we really are. We become immersed in this song and we realize that we have always been intimately involved in its unfoldment. We know now that God is actually singing us into existence, singing all of life into existence and that the song is never-ending.

NOVEMBER 18 -- FORGET -- I am forgetting all lack. Today, as we enter into the quiet place of prayer let us forget what we want. The surface prayers of the past can give way to true prayer. To see past what we think we need, turning those trivial things over to the care of God, we give our problems away and Unity turns them into victories over the suffering of the ego. All of these wants are really idols, to which we turn thinking they can fix us or make us feel better. If we truly let them go, trusting in the love of God, they will all be answered. On the other hand, holding on to them will surely take our focus off of our true living and keep us stuck in lack-consciousness. Where even if these small things are realized we remain unsatisfied, moving from one ego-desire to the next. So right now, let us give all of our wants, needs, problems and questions to God. God will accept them as gifts and turn them into true gifts for us.

NOVEMBER 19 -- LET GO -- I am letting go. We have all heard the saying "Let go and let God." Today we do just that, we take our needs, our obsessions, our concerns and worries and we just let go; we let go of any sense that we need to fix anything. We can do this because we can trust God to care for all of our "issues". Whether they are personal concerns or concerns for others they are all the same to God. So we see ourselves loosening our grip on these various fears, letting them slip away, confident that God will care for them much better than we can from our limited perspective. We visualize ourselves moving gracefully aside, out of the way, so that divine order can be realized in all of our affairs. We wait in silence, knowing that the Love that cares for all the universe will instruct us; letting us know what we should do and when we should do it. We understand the answer may be to do some specific thing or to do nothing at all. It is no longer of any great concern to us, because we have given all concerns over the Care of God and we see that they have all merged into unity.

NOVEMBER 20 -- BETWEEN -- I am not blocked. There is nothing standing between God and us. It is so important to see that we do not need an intermediator to help us communicate with God. There are those who are equal but who temporarily have something that can help us, but we should know that God is directly available to us at any time and in any place. What stands between us are judgments, erroneous views of life which keep us at odds with our fellows and hence with God. When we see the good in our brothers and sisters we acknowledge the Good of God and that removes all of the blocks to that love. As theses fears dissipate, our consciousness raises and we can be sure that we cannot fail to reach God. Having cleansed our sight, we can begin to see the Christ spirit, the Buddha nature of all of those around us; this reminds us that same spirit and nature is in us. We are blocked no longer.

NOVEMBER 21 -- CHRIST -- I am in Christ. I am in Christ and Christ is in me. We are truly the Christ. This is our true identity, our shared identity. To identify with Christ is to identify with Spirit. Identifying with the body has been our biggest stumbling block on our path back to God. "What if that was Jesus?" This is a question that has been asked many times, by many of our brothers and sisters. It usually comes up when we are considering how we should treat someone who has crossed our path. Well the answer to the question is "He was, she was!" Yes, everyone who comes in front of us is Christ and whatever we give to them is what we will simultaneously receive. If we are having trouble seeing the "halo" around our brothers, we can pray that it be revealed to us. A simple request to the Holy Spirit asking that we see what is really there will be answered by a vision of light. If we truly want to see our brothers and sisters as they truly are, we will. The ability to see through any seeming shortcoming will be provided according to our present willingness. This vision is a spiritual sight which has no expectations, no demands, no wants but delivers all that we will ever need.

NOVEMBER 22 - WINGS - I am putting wings on my prayers. Many times we have prayed for freedom from some painful situation. The way to speed the answer to these prayers is forgiveness. Let us take a moment right now to think about the most painful unresolved issue in our lives. Yes, just that fast it comes to mind...now just as fast it can be healed! Get a clear picture of this situation in mind, now picture what life would be like if this problem were solved. The path between the problem and the solution is the path of forgiveness. See the Light of God flowing from your heart, notice how this love enfolds the situation (or person) allow this love to wash clean any dis-ease (upset, anger, fear, anxiety). If it is a situation this is enough...bathed in the light of Life, it is healed. Holy Spirit will provide the answer as to what comes next, if you listen. If it is a person see them totally involved in the light so that you can no longer even discern their features, envision them in the light, of the light and now totally anonymous in Christ. They are now just like every other brother or sister...just like the true you, unencumbered by any problems, mistakes, or anything else that could separate them from you. These are the wings of prayer.

NOVEMBER 23 - REMEDY - I am the remedy. Today any suffering that I observe, I will forgive. I am no longer confused as to what forgiveness is...forgiveness is forgetting. I will allow a healing balm of forgetfulness cover any remembered hurt from the past. Forgiveness is not "letting some one off the hook", it is not saying that the harm done was "not that big a deal", it is not putting up with "bad" behavior. We do not have to "get over it" or let someone "get over" on us. All of these terms are a smoke screen for judgment, and judgment means suffering and separation. I will remedy all suffering and separation simply by seeing that suffering and separation are not real. They are not real in spirit and so they exist only in shadows of my mind. I see the truth, that only Spirit exists and that in Spirit we are all one and that in oneness there is no suffering. I will hold this vision of Light in my mind and I will bring any shadow that comes to me into that light where it will dissipate.

NOVEMBER 24 -- OVERLOOK -- I am overlooking all disturbance. Sooner or later we will all tire in our judgments. Whereas we have focused on noticing conflicts, mistakes, and infractions we can now put all these perceptions aside. Having magnified conflict and error we have increased our own guilt. Choosing to see evil we have sentenced ourselves to shame. We look to punish and we anticipate punishment. Guilt and punishment can truly become things of the past. Look past error, let it remain unreal. Choose to see the love and peace which are present in every moment. Be enlightened, visualize the Buddha nature (Christ presence) in everyone who comes in front of us. This is within our power to select. Overlooking sin means returning to Love, it means forgetting hate. Changing our view, we see creation as it was meant to be. Pure spirit extends everywhere, to everyone, when that is what we are determined to experience. We overlook disturbance and we are at peace.

NOVEMBER 25 -- INNOCENCE -- I am innocent. As we pray to forgive we should know that we are innocent. We are all innocent...all of us...all of our brothers and sisters. All innocent and untouched by error of any kind. When we notice error in others we should immediately recognize that this is but a projection of our own guilt onto those we see around us. Why would we want to see these negative aspects projected on others? We know! We want to see them in others so that we don't see them in ourselves. We believe these sins are our own, but we don't want to face up to them, so we shove them onto others. But what is it that we are trying to escape? Well it is true that in Spirit there is no sin at all, so all of this mental juxtaposition is to no avail. We are trying to get rid of something that is not even there. Still, in this world we can have much happiness by forgiving those mistakes we think we see in others, thereby forgiving ourselves. Find innocence in your brother, in your sister and we will find it in ourselves.

NOVEMBER 26 -- FREE -- I am free. To long have we been prisoners to deception. Look close at the deception and we will see ourselves the deceivers and the deceived. We believed that we are victims of the world, not so; for we created the world we see. We have seen ourselves injured by others, hurt by circumstance and event. We have thought we were subject to a random world and a capricious God. Slaves to anyone we meet, dependent on words and actions of others, we are tethered by codependency. We can free ourselves of this insane vision by releasing our brother from the burden and taking responsibility for our own lives. This is freedom! Know that we experience exactly what we have ordered from life. We are responsible. Everything we have thought, said, done, or left undone has delivered consequences. It may seem harsh, but this is actually our release from the prison of dependence to the freedom of inter-dependence. Let people do what they will. We then can do what we will, and no matter what occurs we remember that it is what we do next that will determine our experience.

NOVEMBER 27 -- NEXUS -- I am at the nexus of creation. This moment is the only moment. It is the nexus of creation. We are always in this moment, really we are. Our minds have wandered that's all. We have allowed our minds to become obsessed with past occurrences, which we then have projected into a fantasy of the future. As each moment unfolds we take the stimulus and filter it through our past experiences choose one that seems to fit and then we order the future to match the past. Therefore, we continue to get the same experiences to one degree or another over and over again. We have been trapped into patterns of behavior which in turn deliver consequences that are limited and limiting. We can see it differently. We can get a fresh look at the present moment by releasing the past. Get quiet, let go of each thought as it occurs, allow time to slow, and finally experience timelessness. All mistakes are gone, the world of conflict fades away, the sight of the eyes is replaced with spiritual vision. Forgiveness allows the erroneous images of the past be replaced with the unchanging view of heaven. Here in the quiet Creation is, here God speaks. From here Creation extends as love and light. It is not necessary to stay seated and unmoving, we can get up and carry this state of mind with us into whatever activity is called for. Go out into the world, to work, to school, or wherever we are guided. Love goes with us and extends from us, creating more love as we stay in the moment and allow ourselves to be inspired by the Voice for God.

NOVEMBER 28 -- HELP -- I am asking for help. The fragmentation that is the insanity of self-centeredness can be healed right now. Locked into the small self only the prison of loneliness is experienced. Escape is possible, help is available. We can ask Spirit to teach us new vision, a sight that sees past error to the purity of God's son. Ask and receive. We have no need greater than this, the ability to see what is really there. To release all of the sick thoughts mired in the past and think with Divine mind thoughts of love and light. Ask for this help right now, and feel God's mercy remove all of the pain of the world. Forgiven it rises to meet us, transformed from blighted desert to verdant garden. Help has come and brought with it the Unity of all Life. The fragments of personality are reunited into the whole that is greater than any personality. The Son of God is indeed one. Should we forget again, no worries, just stop and ask again. Help is available again and again until we no longer need it.

NOVEMBER 29 -- SANE -- I am sane. Sane, it means whole and healthy of mind. Since in reality Mind is all there is, this would seem to say that I am unified with that Mind and in that I am in that Mind. Any sight I see that contradicts unity is a sign that I have left unity and am experiencing some form of insanity. Anytime I feel disconnected from life, I am by definition insane. Let us find no fault in this insanity. It is just a temporary obstacle; we can get back on the right track simply by seeing the truth; that there is no possible way that we can be apart from life…we are always a part of life. God is continually offering this gift of oneness, in order for us to receive it we must be willing to give it. All limitations fall away as we remember our ultimate identity. We are notes in the song of Life that all creation sings endlessly to God.

NOVEMBER 30 -- LEARN -- I am learning. We are learning and in that learning we are changing our perception. We change our perception of the world as a dangerous place where we must always be on guard to a place of safety where we can not be harmed. The more we change our perception, the closer we get to the foot of the bridge that leads to heaven. Learning eventually leads us the place where no more learning is needed...the place of knowledge. We learn that our experiences are either of love or of fear and that the fear is just a lie we tell ourselves. We begin to release fear by forgiving all of the fearful things we tell ourselves. We stand before a locked door that only forgiveness can open. We may be in so much darkness that we cannot even see the door. We must recognize theses shadows as our own self-deceptions. We forgive falsely and then wonder why we keep remembering the hurt. We must stop using false forgiveness as a way through life and start really letting go of all regret and resentment. Clean all thoughts of betrayal from the mind. Let past mistakes disappear in the realization of innocence. Teach forgiveness to learn forgiveness; teach love to learn love.

DECEMBER 1 -- PEACE -- I am at peace. Peace is possible, peace is available, peace is present right now. Living in "bizzaro" world we sometimes cannot even conceive of what peace could be like. Trapped in the world of opposites only conflict seems possible. Know that we can choose what we will. We can will what we choose. The power of choice is present at every moment and in every place. So today the more choices for good we make the more peace we will experience. Presented with the disagreement of another, see instead how easy it is to agree on love. In a moment of lack realize that with each breath we have all that we have already received all that there is. Caught in greed feel the flow of good coming in and going out. Choose to free thought from comparisons and watch how prayer soars. Feeling at odds with anything choose instead to feel reconciliation. We know what all of these experiences are like and we can choose Good anytime we are truly tired of suffering. Choose once again and rise above chaos into peace.

DECEMBER 2 -- WHOLE -- I am seeking wholeness. Perceiving a world in pain, we have sometimes been mislead in our attempts to help. Our misguided charities serve to maintain separation in our minds. Any thought of giving to someone who seems to be or have less than us is highly suspect. Our "help" in these situations are veiled attempts to make ourselves feel superior. These activities exacerbate the loneliness of our lives. The appearance of lack or need should be confronted directly by recognizing that it is just an illusion, a temporary condition that can be healed. The healing comes from forgiveness. True forgiveness sees the whole world whole. So our practice today can be observing wholeness wherever we have perceived fragmentation. To see the light of Unity embracing any and all hurts in a loving, healing balm. To see all outer problems healed by placing them on the alter of God which lies within. This is our joyous work for this day.

DECEMBER 3 -- EQUAL -- I am equal. Today we remember that our help to others is the help of equals giving to equals. When we are guided to be helpful it is not from a lofty position to anothers' lowly position. We recognize that the service we give is a balancing. Temporarily we have more of one thing or another which we are giving to a brother or sister who temporarily has less. This is not some "grand" act designed to make ourselves feel better because we were able to save some poor wretch from their fate. Seen that way we live as arrogant lords in castles of separation...these are the dwellings of ego and they need to be taken down brick by ignorant brick. To see our siblings as "less than" and ourselves as "more than" is just another exercise in self-centeredness. From here there is only more comparison and judgment. Surely we will see ourselves as "less than" and some other as "more than" and then reversed in some way because we cannot stand for it. Let us start now, today to free ourselves from these crazy images by freeing all of those around us. We are equal, say it now, we are all equal.

DECEMBER 4 -- SINLESS -- I am sinless. We are sinless. The old paradigm of universal sinfulness is the tool of egos trying to keep other egos in check. It feigns brotherhood, but a brotherhood which is mired in error. "Sinners all, not one of us worthy of the love of God." This is an attempt to say that our equality lies in our defects. A spark of false hope is given in the offering of some personal salvation for those of us who ask "Jesus" to come into them. Here again is separation celebrated and made "real". United in sin but capable of going separately to some strange heaven where only some are allowed eternal life. This of course is the ultimate superiority. All of these deceptions are designed to keep us from remembering our true identity. A loving God would not allow such things to be real. God created us perfect and without blemish. The kingdom of heaven is our eternal home. None can be barred because then it would not be complete, which is impossible because Heaven is the kingdom of One-ness in which no separation exists. We are son of God, and as such we are sinless.

DECEMBER 5 -- MARTYR -- I am released from martyrdom. Martyrdom is the ultimate ego trip. For the martyred it is a monument to their sacrifice. For the witness it is a cause for revenge. Both of these are exercises in futility and suffering. Today we stop accepting the enmity of others. In the past we may have simply suffered in silence when injury seemed to be offered from our brothers. This is not helpful...we still feel the hurt and witness the injustice and then take on the role of the sacrificed. Focus instead on seeing things differently, let the hurt of those who offer injury be healed along with the injured, for surely they are the same. Recognize only the light in all, see how the darkness dissipates before it. Forget the injury in truth and in light. See it fading away before the love of God. No one guilty, no one sacrificed, none to suffer...this is the path of forgiveness, the path back to our true Home.

DECEMBER 6 -- BARGAIN -- I am free of bargains. We are not here to bargain with one another for our perceived wants and needs. We are here to give freely without conditions. Compromise is the slavery of expectations. We have made contracts with those around us that we will act in certain ways as long as others act in similar ways. Many times these agreements have not even been made known to the other person. We have set the expectations in our mind and then we judge against them. As long as someone goes along with our terms we treat them with some measure of kindness, but should they transgress they are punished. Today we release everyone from former bargains and let them be. In that release lies our own freedom as well as the freedom of the world. Now we can give the way we are designed to give...without thought of reward. The gift is in the giving. Now we are free to be who we really are and we have freed our brothers and sisters to be likewise.

DECEMBER 7 -- HAPPY -- I am happy. God's will is for our happiness. Yes, God wants us to be happy. In this world it can be difficult, but a way has been provided for us. We have a mission and purpose in this life that will provide our happiness. Our purpose here is to give of ourselves. Suffering comes from giving of our small self...our ego self, where in our fear we can give only treachery and pain. Happiness comes from giving from our divine Self. Proper service is our mission, doing the right thing, for the right reason and exactly the right time. This means that any action we take needs to be for the common good and that we are motivated only by goodwill and because of the first two our timing is impeccable. Our happiness comes directly from our giving that which we are (ourselves)...that which we are is that which our Father made: simply Love. So, we will be happy in the giving of love which is all we are and really all we have to give.

DECEMBER 8 -- UNAFRAID -- I am unafraid. Today we release all fear. Fear is anger, condemnation and comparison...each a little death reflecting the big death which in separation we both loathe and worship. The emotional roller coaster of reaction is a poor substitute for the peace of God. We have a divine identity which we have tried to mask with these petty attributes. The Christ is in us all. The Christ is for us all. The Christ mind is the state in which we come together with all life, forgiving any appearance of threat. All the deceptions of the ego are put aside. No longer do we need the dubious rewards of judgment. We can see the light of love everywhere, in everyone and in everything. All are redeemed when we move out of the shadows and in that Light. We see ourselves free to rise on shining wings from all that has bound us to the dark earth. Lifted up we envision the real world glowing, emanating love, a paradise where all conflict, fear and dread have been healed.

DECEMBER 9 -- SALVATION -- I am saved? We either share salvation or there is none. It is our choice but to have it we must share it. We must take everyone with us, or not one can go. No requirements are made, no conditions asked. We are the agents of salvation in this world. We are ministers of God and as such we are ministers of God's will, goodwill. Trust in God must mean trust in our brothers and ourselves since we are all of God. As we go through this day there will be someone who we interact with that we will see as offensive in some way, large or small it does not matter. Recognize this person, this one in front you, recognize that they are your savior. Seeing the presence of Christ in them will lead you to the recognition of the presence of Christ in you. This is truly salvation when one part of God saves another part by seeing that there are really no separate parts, only the wholeness of God. We are saved in the common salvation of us all. So, yes it is true we are saved in Christ.

DECEMBER 10 -- FORM -- I am forming my life. We are forming the world we see. Through our choices our world is made. As we decide the course we will take, we become the cause of our life experience. Our single purpose here in this world is to be helpful. Being truly helpful we heal the perceived gaps between ourselves and our brothers. Opportunities arise with each meeting...people come before us and we are called to see them correctly, to forgive any judgment we may make. We should not decide for ourselves what the form of that correction should take. We allow the Holy Spirit to take charge of our perceptions. Listening to Spirit our thinking begins to change, our actions take on the mantle of love, and our resulting life experience is one that moves us closer and closer to the foot of the bridge that spans the gap to heaven. So today choose spirit, choose loving service and watch how the world changes.

DECEMBER 11 -- TASK -- I am guided in my task. Today let us question our role in the lives of our brothers and sisters. Our inquiry will be best answered by asking Spirit what to do. Opening ourselves to guidance means letting go of our own opinions of what our fellows need. We take all of our ideas and just put them aside, clearing the way for a divine answer. This can be accomplished in a second. In a moment, in a holy instant we can connect to our inner guide and become quite clear as to the best course of action. We can be confident in the guidance when we realize that the answer is good for everyone involved. Looking to the light in each one, we wash away any imperfections in ourselves and in them. We release ourselves and all others from the burdens of past events. Quiet and calm we allow ourselves to hear the answer from the One whose function it is to provide it. Then without worry or anxiety of any kind we put the guidance into action.

DECEMBER 12 -- HEAR -- I am hearing the Voice for God. As we quiet the mind today, we are opening the way for Spirit to be heard. This inner guide is always present but many times we have ignored the call; many times we have been distracted by the plaintiff cries of ego. As we practice stillness we are putting those distractions to the side so that we can clearly hear the still, small voice of Truth. Today we will hear the word of Peace, the word of wholeness, the word of health. We will be shown the unreality of sin and guilt and even death. Our place in God is revealed, our function of forgiveness shown, listening we hear it all. Call to Him now and He will reveal, give Him all of your worries and concerns. The Way will be made clear, Love leads us from the grasping, clutching life of lack into the generous and abundant consciousness of giving. All judgment fades as we become more and more open to the message of Unity that flows from within. A door has opened into the kingdom of Heaven, stand a moment and bask in its light. Notice your brother standing in the Rays that reveal our true, shared identity.

DECEMBER 13 -- AIDED -- I am aided in my quest. Yes, our task is to help. Our work is to give proper service, and this may sometimes seem to be overwhelming. Relax, be calm and know that in the help we seek to give there is help for us. All around us are helpers, some visible to our physical eye but most discernible only to spirit. Angels all, divine ideas, words of God coming to help us in our unfolding mission. We would return to Love, return to One-ness, remember God. On this journey we give to our companions, but we also receive from them...it cannot be otherwise. Sometimes we forget that every act is reciprocal. Know it now, everything we have need of is being provided. It is not up to us alone, because we can never really be alone. Look to the help that is available, ask for it and take it.

DECEMBER 14 -- WELL -- I am well. Sickness is an effect. Anytime we are sick, we have become the victim of our own making. Illness is a symbol of the separation which of course is original sin, the only sin and our only problem. This sin has shown itself as disease.... dis-ease. This is also the nature of the body which we have also made...disharmony, disruption, finally dissolution.... the body will die. The body is a temporary refuge from our guilt, an attempt to forget our true form...it is designed to fall apart and then come back to this world in a somewhat altered form. It is not real; it is not us. We can choose something different and if we do the body will reflect this different choice, but still, eventually it will fall to dust. It is the sin that must be forgiven for us to escape this cycle of life and death. Of course even this sin which seems the most severe, the act of leaving God and apparently fighting against God, is just illusion. So, the shadow of this ultimate error is a just a shadow of a shadow...as such it can be brought to light and then true healing occurs.

DECEMBER 15 -- IMMORTAL -- I am immortal. We, as Spirit are immortal, the body is not. Remarkably though, we can heal the body as a result of forgiveness. When we remember the immortality that is our inheritance we radiate love which has great effect upon all bodies. By overlooking the symptoms of age and entropy we can actually ameliorate them. Our bodies rush to death, destruction can be slowed for a time but we must also remember that it must be laid aside at some time. This need not be a cause for concern when we stay aware that we are not our bodies, but rather we are immortal Spirit....that no matter what appears to be happening in the world, we are above the world, we indeed have overcome the world. When we focus on the fact that the body cannot hold the real us in a prison of flesh we can be kinder to it, forgiving any grievances that we have against it. Seeing it as it is, a communications device which allows us to interact with our brothers and sisters in a loving way.

DECEMBER 16 -- REMEMBER – I am remembering. Somewhere deep within us we can remember eternal life, we are always and have always been part of eternal life. The life we have been experiencing in this world is not the genuine article, but rather some pale imitation. We have imagined ourselves with bodies that sicken and wither and eventually die. This is a shadow existence which cannot reflect the truth of our being. Remembering though, remembering the Glory which is our Source, brings us a measure of peace, health and wholeness even here. So when the shadows appear today we can overlook them, putting our minds back into alignment with divine mind. Casting thoughts back to our original state, the state of mind in which there is nothing but love, nothing but unabbreviated unending life. As we remember eternity we bring peace, health and wholeness to our body and to the world of bodies. We bring healing to our brothers and to ourselves.

DECEMBER 17 -- OPPOSITES -- I am true. Today we focus on healing the world of opposites. There is a real world here that can be seen if we are willing. Through the release of judgment, we can see a garden of love in place of the desert of fear. Every experience will be an opportunity for healing. Begin with purpose, remember that our function here is to forgive and to extend love. People will come before us all day and night...and when they do it is our cue to forgive. Just notice how they appear; do we see their shortcomings, do we notice their imperfections, are we remembering their sins of the past? Whatever darkness we have seen in them we can bring to the light whenever we choose. All of the contrasts, all of the opinions we see concerning these brothers and sisters are just distractions that keep us from seeing the truth. Where we see opposites we can see Unity...this is the key to healing. It is bringing the fragments of life back into wholeness. So whatever imperfections we are focused on we can visualize the Light of God acting as restoration. See each brother being given to the Light and marvel as all of the past is washed away in a healing wave of forgiving forgetfulness. They stand before us now genuine and true...reminding us that we are likewise.

DECEMBER 18 -- LIFE -- I am alive with the Life of God. Our true life is not the life of the body which we now seem to inhabit, we are actually alive in God, in Spirit and that life is eternal. The life of the body is temporary and imperfect; the Life of Spirit is infinite and perfect. In the worldly experience we have pain and sickness which leads to the eventual death of the body. We can through prayer or medicine lessen the suffering and even experience healing of a sort...the problem is that we replace one sickness with another and still the body dies. This condition of the world we see is one that causes great fear. Our best solution is to realize and admit that this body will not last but that which lies beyond the body is everlasting and our true existence. Once this idea is firmly implanted we can begin to let go of our attachment to the physical and be at peace with the transition that is to come. From this perspective much less physical discomfort is felt, our bodies still age but with more grace, sickness and disease are easily set aside when we have no fear of them. When the time comes we are able to simply take our bodies "off" and lay them down like worn out clothes. No struggle, no suffering only peace...

DECEMBER 19 -- HUMILITY -- I am humble. In humility we are equal. It just means that we know who we are and we don't have to act like something else. In the past we may have thought that our identity was quite mundane and then made silly attempts to appear greater. Rather than being less than adequate we are really quite divine. We are brothers and sisters in the Christ spirit.... indeed, we are children of God. This perspective is quite different from our previous view. In humility then, we see ourselves as Son of God, which is perfect. Of course this also means that everyone else is likewise perfect. So, being humble means being equal. What a freeing idea, no one greater and no one lesser...all of us divine parts of a divine whole...and each of us irreplaceable.

DECEMBER 20 -- HEALER -- I am healing. As we remember where we come from and who is our Creator we become the healed and the healer. We are able to alleviate suffering in ourselves and those who come to us. Everyone we meet can be brought into Unity with us. By extending love to our brothers and sisters we set the stage for health and wholeness. We affirm that we are one with all and that the love of God is moving in and through us. Having established the truth, we share it with anyone who has a need. The conscious contact with God that is available to us all leads us to give as required. We see our brothers whole; we see them perfect, without blemish. We give them to the light of Creation knowing that their absolute health is assured.

DECEMBER 21 -- PEACE -- I am at peace. Today as we quiet the mind and calm the body a great peace flows over us. We are connected to all of life; all life is connected to us, and all is well. There is no worry, no want and no need. If any of these should occur to us, we simply give these concerns to God and return to our center. Know that in this state we can do nothing but bring peace to every mind that touches ours. We can carry this peace out of our meditation and into the world. By watching carefully in each moment we keep ourselves connected and at rest. We become peace-makers wherever we go and with whomever we meet. Although this seems like a special state it is really just a hint of our original state, but still this clue to our identity has the power to bring light to the shadows of this world. Be at peace this day and observe how it flows between us and everyone we perceive in a healing tide love.

DECEMBER 22 -- WITNESS -- I am witness to love. Forgiveness' opportunity lies at every turn this day. See yourself moving through this day one moment at a time, paying attention to each one...seeing only good and light and love. At times we may be tempted to look upon strife, war, and suffering with fear and foreboding; but instead we see only the call for love. We respond to each call for love with the extension of love from our hearts...the world responds by reflecting this love back to us. Witness the coming of the light...the light that banishes the darkness. This light, so bright that the material world itself is shined into Eden and finally into Heaven itself. Witness this, witness for this; see love and express love, give love and receive love. And then you can say "I saw the whole thing, I am a witness!"

DECEMBER 23 -- HOLY -- I am very holy? We are very holy. Today we help Christ consciousness be established in all of our endeavors. We remember the one goal of forgiveness. We see our sanity restored and with us all living things brought back to our original oneness. Joy is upon us as we feel the completion of our ancient goal. We are sharing in the Love of God, basking in the Light of Spirit, immersed in the Forgiveness of Christ. We will except nothing less than wholeness in this precious moment. We have let go of every want knowing that what we receive in return is much greater. We are very holy...we are very holy as we forgive any seeming lack. We remember to forgive, we remember to forget, and we are very holy indeed!

DECEMBER 24 -- PRAY -- I am praying as I go. We pray as we go. Focusing on the present we can maintain an attitude of forgiveness that opens the way to true prayer which in turn heals any seeming upset. So first forgiveness... it means to see a thing differently, to release any past images and see in the light of Spirit. Then prayer...an affirmation of only good for all involved, a turning over of all expectations, and a stepping aside. Then healing comes, wholeness is re-established...health restored. One with the wellspring of all Life we flow into world as healers, extending and giving the gift of Love to all whom we meet. Staying in this day, living in this moment, focusing on right now we are healed and we are healing. Our prayers rise up to their divine potential, which is to say perfection! Forgiving, praying, healing as we go...and in this way we go together.

DECEMBER 25 - GENEROSITY - I am generous. We can only keep what we have by giving it away. This seems to fly in the face of worldly thinking. Obviously if I have a certain thing and then I give this thing away I will not have it anymore. The gifts of Spirit however can never be lost. When we truly give of ourselves we receive all that we give and more. "To have all give all to all." This is a quote from the workbook of A Course in Miracles which has been a cause for concern among many students. It is referring to the Gift of Self to Self. It is not concerned with the conditional gifts of the material world. This principle is the total relinquishment of ourselves into the whole of Life. We may ask where this leaves us concerning material things. Well first they are temporary and not of any real value, but we must remember that all things in the world can be reflections of Heaven. So, the ability to give what we have in the world is a talent we should reinforce. We could say that we should not accept gifts that we could not bear to turn around and give to someone else because then they would be a hindrance to our ongoing. Be generous and know that all things are provided.

DECEMBER 26 -- CHILD -- I am Child of God. We are the Son of God...together we are the Son of God. This is our choice: "A part of" we exist in harmony with all of life, "apart from" we see only disharmony. Today, let us choose our birthright, let us choose Unity. We also remember our place...we are the created. God created us thus giving us the ability to create. Don't get the roles reversed...we are a thought in the mind of God...we exist in God. We did not create God, but we can create through the love of God of which we are made. We can become cause in our life but we can never be the cause of God. Picture yourself at the oceans shore, taking a cup you have brought with you bend down and scoop some of the water into the cup. Looking now at the cup filled with ocean water you do not confuse this small amount with the entire ocean. So with us...we spring from God and have attributes of God but while we are in the "cup" we are not the whole ocean.

DECEMBER 27 -- ARISE -- I am rising. Today, we rise up in consciousness. We consciously raise our thoughts to God. We arise from all illness. Let us dream a happy dream...let us dream of healing and then awaken whole and healthy. We release any dark thoughts concerning sickness; we let go of all disease, dysfunction, or disorder of body or mind. We feel at home, perfect and serene. All thoughts of threat or attack, want or lack fade into the light of God. We give up wandering from one painful scenario to another. We give all suffering into the hands of Spirit and we are guided into joy and bliss. Centered in our quiet, inner sanctuary we are free from darkness and death...we have arisen into Unity and Love.

DECEMBER 28 -- RECALLED -- I am recalled to heaven. God is calling us back into the kingdom right now. The kingdom of heaven is not the land of the dead...it is actually the home of Life. So, not a place to go after the body dies but a state of mind that is available right now in which all life is eternally one. It is our natural place and we are most welcome there. It is the habitation of peace (Jerusalem) in which forever we attain our true identity. The voice for God speaks to us at all times and in all places...calling us back into awareness of our birthright. We are children of God and as such we inherit the kingdom of God. For too long we have languished here in the shadows of the material world. Make a point today to listen for the still small voice of God which is really speaking to us in all places and at all times. Listen and be recalled to paradise.

DECEMBER 29 -- REMINDED -- I am reminded of eternity. Our true place is in the eternal realm of our Creator. Our Father is waiting for our remembrance. The kingdom is not complete without us. The song of life cannot be sung without our participation. As we get quiet today, let us attempt to remember our ancient place. Let us hear the singing of angels and add our voice to the harmony. Our combined music is at work right now awakening our brothers and sisters from their slumber...reminding them of our place in this cosmic symphony. Heaven's melody rings clear in our hearts, vibrating with the love that wipes away the chaotic clangor of fear. Beyond space/time we exist in everlasting life; our song is the extension of love and life which rings forever down the halls of eternity.

DECEMBER 30 -- CREATION -- I am creative. Creation is extending. Love extends strength to us and then we extend love back. The heavy load we carry in the material world is the shadow of the heavy load of fear that world itself carries. Creation, the extension of love, manifests itself as all of the qualities that we need to move through our experiences in this world with calm and peaceful purpose. Happiness is available right now. Creation is speaking joy to us in this moment, hear it saying: "You are my perfect child." Make a gift to God in this moment; give him all of your worries and concerns, hear him say: "This gift I receive with love and thereby turn it to Love." In this way are all of our distractions forgiven and made peaceful. In this way our efforts in the world change from burdens of responsibility to joys of privilege. Creation is extending through us giving us the ability to give our various gifts to the world. As we continue to give with love our perception of this place changes from conflict to harmony. Whereas we saw a desert we now see a garden.

DECEMBER 31 -- RETURN -- I am returning to Love. We can return to Love. The song of prayer echoes in our hearts, today we can sing out; allowing this music of Light be heard throughout our world and throughout the universe. Freedom is ours as soon as we accept it, we are free to be and to do. To be our true selves, to do our part in the restoration of sanity. Our part right now is kindness. Focus on being kind...be kind to the whole world, be kind to us, be kind to God...yes be kind to God. In our fearful existence we have feared God and that which is feared must be hated on some level. So when we extend that kindness to our our environment, to our brothers and ourselves, think bigger think God. The return to love in is the awareness that love is all there is. Love is the stuff that we are made of and it is the stuff that our Maker is made of. So as we are kind, we are expressing that which is our true self and the true Self of God thereby remembering and returning to the Oneness of Love.

Printed in the United States
By Bookmasters